God and His Final Messenger

Makkan Period

Introduces the life of the Final Prophet and the main events that depict his role as the last Messenger of God on Earth. The attributes and sunnah of God (how He deals with human beings) will be introduced at appropriate places to illustrate how God intervenes in our lives, as He did in the Prophet's life. This level will cover the Makkan period.

**Ghamidi Center
of Islamic Learning**
www.ghamidi.org   AN INITIATIVE OF AL-MAWRID US.

Publisher: Ghamidi Center of Islamic Learning - Al-Mawrid US
ISBN: 978-1-966600-26-8

Address: 3620 N Josey Ln, Suite 230 Carrollton, TX 75007
Website: www.ghamidicenter.com
Email: info@ghamidi.org

Chapter 1

Introduction to the Course

This chapter introduces the course and its objectives.

Introduction

- The Quran has made the obedience of Prophet Muhammad a condition for loving God and receiving His love and forgiveness (Surah 3, Verse 31).

- A hadith narrated by Anas ibn Malik implies that loving Prophet Muhammad reflects one's perfection of faith (Sahih Al-Bukhari 15, Muslim 44).

- Loving God and His messenger, and obeying them, are part of our religion. However, can we claim to have a deep, sincere love for someone without knowing them?

- This two-part course is unique in that it seeks to introduce God and His final messenger by studying the messenger's life on earth, known as Seerah. Through this course, we will learn how his life accurately depicted the Quranic teachings, how he lived, and how God manifested His being, commands, and practices through His final messenger. This way, we will learn relevant attributes of God as we study Seerah.

- Studying the Seerah of Prophet Muhammad and how God accompanied him throughout his life will help us build true love for him and his Lord, who is our Lord.

- The content of this course is drawn from the Quran and other authentic sources.

- The course is divided into two parts: the first will focus on the life of the Prophet Muhammad in Makkah until his migration to Medinah, also known as the Makkan period.

- The second part of this course will focus on the life of Prophet Muhammad in Medinah till his departure from this earth, also known as the Medinan period.

Course Objectives

- To get to know our God, Allah (the Most High), and His Final Messenger, Prophet Muhammad (Peace be upon him), through studying the life of the Messenger and how Allah helped him throughout the mission given to him as a Messenger.

- Describe the key events in the life of Prophet Muhammad after he was made a messenger while he lived in Makkah.

- Understand how a messenger and his companions go through different stages and the challenges of the mission until they complete it.

What is Seerah?

In the Arabic language, it comes from the word "Sara," which means to be on a journey

- Seerah is an area of Islamic knowledge where we study the life of Prophet Muhammad:
    - His biography.
    - Events related to his life.
    - Events related to his mission.
    - His relationships as a human being.
    - His habits, preferences, likes, dislikes.
    - And many other aspects of his life.
- His companions tried to preserve his life history, which reached us through narrations called Hadith.
- The Quran also tells us some parts of the life of Prophet Muhammad, but not the complete life.

Important

The primary source of Seerah is Ahadith.

Hadith: A collection of the sayings, actions, and approvals of the Prophet and any matter related to his life reported by the people around him. Ahadith is the plural of Hadith.

What is Hadith?

- Prophet Muhammad's companions lived with him, talked to him, saw him, observed him, asked him questions, spent day and night with him, and then some of them recorded them so they could benefit from them later.
- Some of these people (red and orange in color in the picture below) will go out and recount all this to others who were not present.
- These people narrate their stories to others, and this continues. This knowledge base is Hadith.
- Historians took these narrations from different times, compiled them, and verified them to some extent
- Later historians also benefit from the work of individual narrators and previous historians.

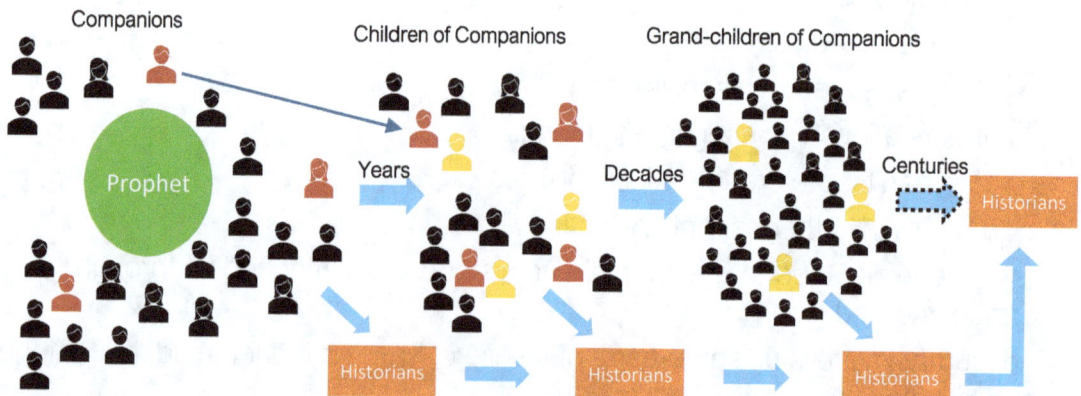

Knowing how narrations were transmitted, it is possible that something was not transmitted correctly or that someone fabricated something about the Prophet. Do you know what the early scholars of Islam did to handle this problem?

Importance of studying the Seerah

The importance

- It is natural to want to know more about the person whom we claim to love.
- It increases our love for him, which is required for our faith.
- In the Quran, events are briefly mentioned, but the Seerah provides more detail.
- We learn from his life and moral behavior and try our best to emulate them.
- The more we know about him, the more we can educate people around us about his character.

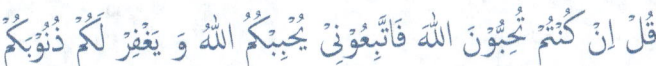

Aisha reported: "Verily, the character of the Prophet of Allah was the Quran." (Sahih Muslim 746)

Our relationship with the Prophet

- Our relationship with the Prophet is: Believe, love, and obey. The Quran described this relationship in this beautiful verse:

قُلْ اِنْ كُنْتُمْ تُحِبُّوْنَ اللهَ فَاتَّبِعُوْنِيْ يُحْبِبْكُمُ اللهُ وَ يَغْفِرْ لَكُمْ ذُنُوْبَكُمْ

Say, (O Muhammad to Muslims), if you really love Allah, then follow me; Allah will love you and will forgive your sins (3:31)

- Prophet Muhammad is now the only source of guidance from Allah.
- It is our duty and part of our faith to learn and understand how Allah and His final messenger want us to live our daily lives.
- This life is a test of our moral character, and Prophet Muhammad's character is the best example for us.
- The best way to earn the pleasure of Allah and become closer to Him is through following the Prophet.

The phases of Prophet's Life

- The life of Prophet Muhammad can be divided into three distinct phases:
  - Before prophethood
  - Makkan period
  - Madinan period
- Although as Muslims we look at his life after he was made a Prophet of God, his life before Prophethood is equally important to study.
- When reading the Quran, we can easily notice that the message and themes of the Quranic Surahs differ between the Makkan and Madinan periods.
- His challenges and enemies in Makkah and Madinah were also very different.

Prophet Muhammad's Age = 63 Years

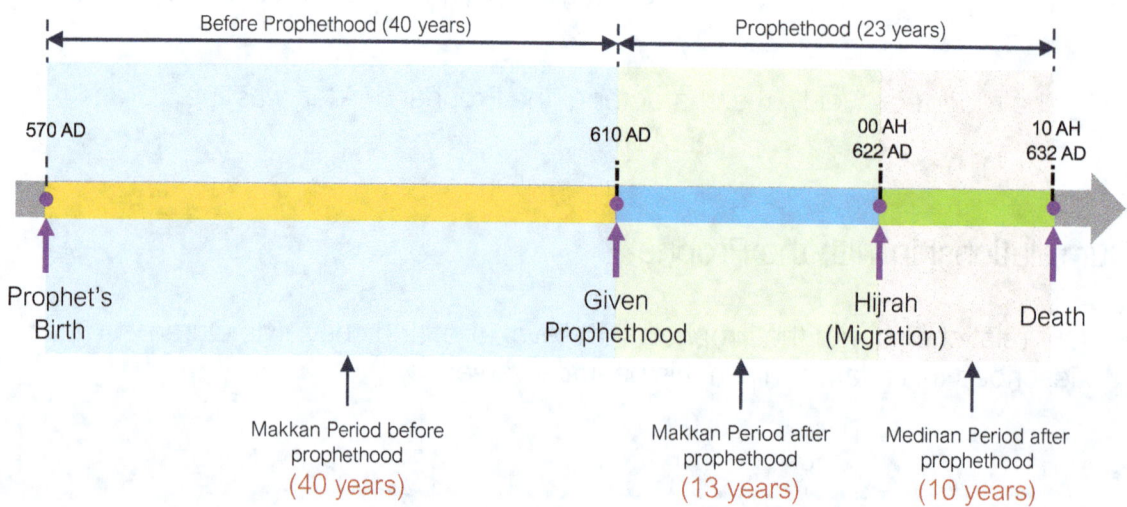

In Level 2, we will study the Makkan period of the Prophet's life. This includes 40 years before Prophethood and 13 years after Prophethood.

God: His attributes and practices

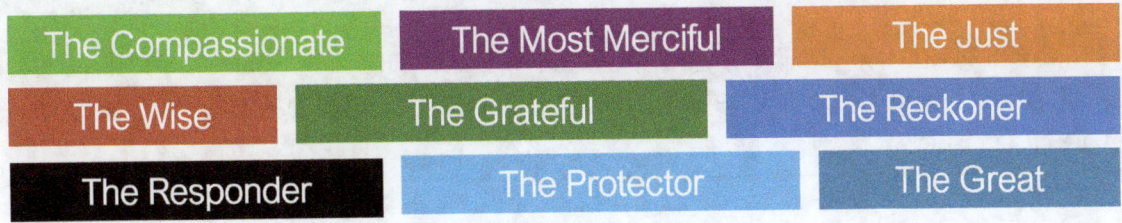

The Compassionate	The Most Merciful	The Just
The Wise	The Grateful	The Reckoner
The Responder	The Protector	The Great

The Quran clearly states about God:

There is nothing that resembles Him (in this world) (42:11)

- As mentioned in the introduction, in this course, we will learn about our God, Allah, and His attributes.
- We do not know Allah's physical person (his being); we can only know Him through His attributes.
- The best way to know God is to see how He deals with us and this world. This is visible through His attributes.
- The Prophet went through many phases and faced many hardships throughout his life, but God always remained with him in every difficult time.
- God showed His attributes and practices throughout the life of Prophet Muhammad.
- We face many difficulties and challenges in our modern lives. By learning about what the Prophet Muhammad did in the face of adversity, challenges, rejection, grief, and loss, we can find answers and strategies to cope. Our circumstances may be very different from those of that time, but we can still find many inspirations for modern life in the Prophet's example and take practical lessons from it.
- Similarly, Prophet's life is the best way to gain a clear understanding of God's attributes and to build a strong relationship with Him.

Activities

Throughout this course, you will complete various Seerah Activities. Activities must be completed and submitted to the teacher in class on the due date.

Important notes

- Throughout the course, the words God and Allah are used interchangeably.
- For brevity and editing, the salutations for the Prophet Muhammad, PEACE BE UPON HIM, are not repeated. But it is highly encouraged that whenever we say or read his name, we send him salutations.

Class instructions

- You are required to attend all classes unless you have a valid reason to skip.
- Please send a note (or ask your parents) to your teacher on Google Classroom if you will skip a session.
- Attendance will be taken at the beginning of every class. Arriving in class 5 minutes after the start will be counted as tardy.
- Three (3) tardies will be counted as one absence.
- Attendance will be counted toward your final assessment.
- Every student will be assessed via:
  - Participation in the class
  - Multiple Quizzes
  - Assignments
  - Semester Exam
  - End-of-Year Exam

SEERAH ACTIVITY

ARABIC CALLIGRAPHY COMPETITION

Pick one name of Allah other than Allah and create a
Colored Calligraphy Artwork by hand (Example below)

Instructions

- Be creative and try to create your own art without copying from the internet.

- Pick an attribute/name of Allah that you love the most.

- The artwork should not be smaller than a standard paper size (11 x 8).

- You can add a theme, graphics, or a picture related to the attributes of Allah.

Chapter 2

Prophets and Messengers

This chapter introduces the concepts of Prophets and Messengers in Islam, their differences, and the roles they play in religion.

Why did Allah send Prophets?

Prophets are Allah's chosen people who remind people of the message of Allah, give good news about the Hereafter to those who accept it, and warn those who reject it.

- Allah's plan is to give us a good life in the Hereafter, while life on earth is temporary and a test.
- Human beings are weak and forget the teachings of Allah easily.
- We are constantly reminded of the true purpose of this life through prophets.
- Our behavior towards Allah's Message and the people around us is the subject of our test.
- That's why the Quran calls Prophets "**Mubashireen**" (bearers of good news) and "**Munzereen**" (warners of the punishment.

The first Prophet Adam and his test

- Adam was the first Prophet of Islam and the first human being on Earth.
- Adam and his wife were put through a test, but Shaytan successfully tricked them and convinced them to disobey Allah.

Test of Obedience   Pass  OR  Fail

- Through Adam, Allah taught us that there would be several tests in this life, all about obeying Allah.
- The main lesson of that story was that our biggest enemy is Shaytan, who wants us to fail, and he would make every effort to remove us from the path of obedience to Allah.

Prophets, Nations and Revelation

- Allah has sent Prophets to every nation since the time of Adam.
- When Allah decides to 'send' a Prophet to a nation, He chooses someone from among the people of that nation.
- A person knows his people, nation, and tribe much better than anyone else.
- When people reject the Prophet, one of two situations arises:
  - The Prophet leaves the world, and nothing happens.
  - Allah punishes the nation in front of him for others to take a lesson (this occurs when the Prophet is made a Messenger).
- Some of the Prophets that are mentioned in the Quran are:

Adam	Idrees	Nuh	Hud	Saleh
Ibrahim	Ismail	Ishaq	Lut	Dawood
Suleiman	Zakariah	Yaqoob	Isa	Muhammad

Revelation sent to the Prophets

- Revelations from Allah to His Prophets are meant to answer these questions exactly. Without revelation, everyone will come up with their own answer, unaware of what is right.

Allah

Revelations

Prophet

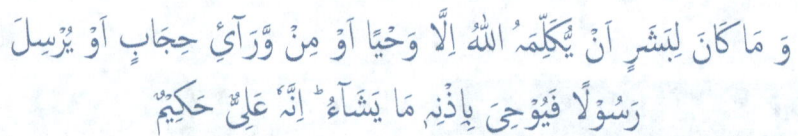

وَ مَا كَانَ لِبَشَرٍ اَنْ يُّكَلِّمَهُ اللهُ اِلَّا وَحْيًا اَوْ مِنْ وَّرَآئِ حِجَابٍ اَوْ يُرْسِلَ رَسُوْلًا فَيُوْحِيَ بِاِذْنِهٖ مَا يَشَآءُ ۚ اِنَّهٗ عَلِيٌّ حَكِيْمٌ

[And it is not appropriate for any human being that Allah should speak to him <u>except</u> by revelation or from behind a veil or that He sends a messenger to reveal, by His permission, what He wills. Indeed, He is Most High and Wise.] (42:51)

- Wahi means to put divine words into the heart or to give a divine message through signs to a human being.
- Wahi is usually sent to the Prophets/Messengers directly or through angels.

Revelation and Divine Books

- Allah gives Divine Books to His Prophets so people have written instructions on matters that are not clear to them, and they can use those instructions to resolve differences.

Prophet Musa (Moses)	Prophet Dawood (David)	Prophet Isa (Jesus)	Prophet Muhammad
		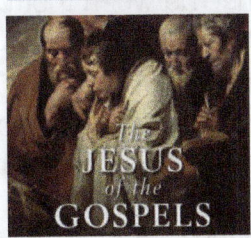	

Prophets help us in our faith

- Some knowledge is built into our nature, and no special guidance is needed in these matters.
- But then the Prophets help us with the details of that knowledge and become the best model for us when practicing the religion of God.
- Prophets become a sign of God and His existence. They strengthen our faith.
- Below is a quick summary of what we know from our nature and how Prophets strengthen that knowledge.

We are a creation	Bring clarity and details on this knowledge in the form of laws
There must be one Creator who created all this	Resolve differences among people through Books
We know what is right and wrong	Help us grow in our commitment to faith
The accountability	They act as the best model for us to follow in religion

Imagine you don't have the Quran, where would you learn the following information from: Who is our God, what does He want from me, what happens after we die, why do I feel bad when I do bad?

Difference between Prophet & Messenger

- People often use the terms "Prophets" and "Messengers" interchangeably, but they are two distinct positions with different roles.
- The Arabic for Prophet is "*Nabi*," and the Messenger is "*Rasool*".
- Scholars of Islam have offered different definitions of a Prophet and a Messenger, and what is the difference between them. However, a careful reader of the Quran can see the difference between them by paying attention to the text and the various examples of Messengers it presents.
- One very popular opinion about the distinction is that the Prophets are not given any new book or the law, while the Messengers are given the book and the law. However, we know that Prophet Daud was a Prophet and he was given a book. Similarly, Prophet Isa was a Messenger, and although he was given a book, he was asked to follow the law of Moses (Torah).

Prophet (Nabi)	Messenger (Rasool)
• "Nabi" means a person who brings important news. • Main message: Oneness of Allah and accountability on the Day of Judgment. • Many prophets have been sent in the past, and at times more than one has been sent to the same nation. • They deliver their message and leave the world as any other person would. • Examples: Prophet Idrees, Prophet Zakariah, Prophet Yahya, Prophet Haroon.	• They do what Nabi does with an additional responsibility of *Risalah*. • They tell their nation that Allah will punish them on this earth after he leaves for not accepting him as a Messenger. This is a special law. • The punishment, through this law, comes on the disbelievers through natural disasters or the Messenger's companions, and the believers are saved. • Examples: Prophet Nuh, Prophet Hud, Prophet Saleh, Prophet Lut, Prophet Isa, Prophet Muhammad (they were all called *Rasool*).

God's law of conclusive communication of the Truth

- Let's look at the law that is special to the Messengers and their nations. The law in Arabic is called *"Qanoon-e-Itmam Al-Hujjah" (the conclusive communication of the Truth)*.
- The law comprises an extended mission given to the Messenger, which defines the different phases of that mission.
- The Messenger must complete the mission and cannot abandon it under any circumstances.
- God guides all the Phases of the mission.
- The various phases of that mission are described here:

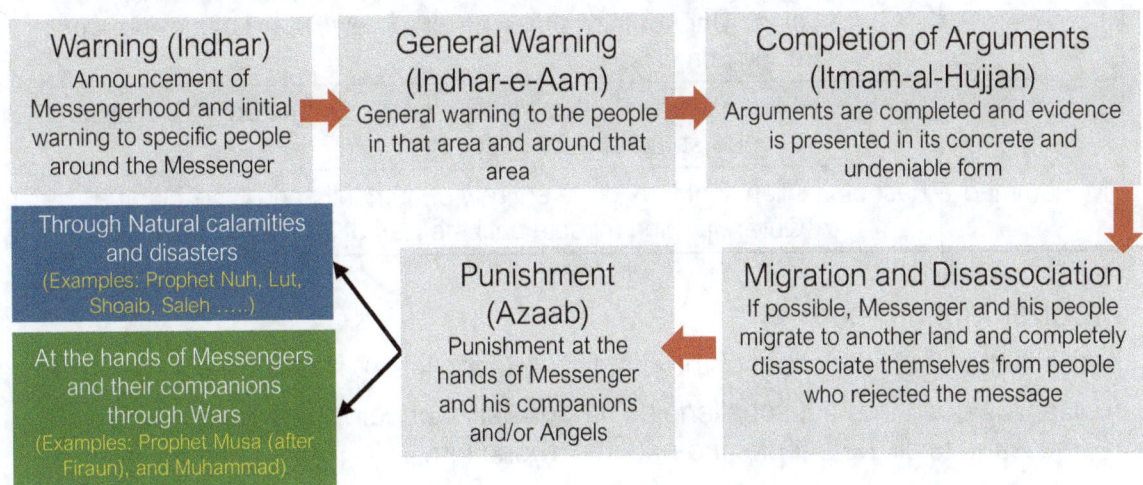

- In the case of Prophet Muhammad, God separated non-believers from believers before the punishment as per His Law. He announced in the Quran that all associations must be severed.
- Then the Polytheists were killed (through wars), and the People of the Book were overpowered and forced to pay tax (Jizyah through wars).
- In the case of Prophet Nuh, he was asked to take his followers on a ship, and the rest of the nation was killed through heavy floods (natural disaster).

Famous Prophets and Messengers

Name	Role	Merits
Adam	Nabi	Allah talked to him directly, the first human being with a human soul/self.
Ibrahim	Rasool	Allah chose him as the leader/father of the nations/prophets after him.
Musa	Rasool	Allah spoke to him and also bestowed upon him unique miracles.
Jesus	Rasool	Allah raised him to the heavens and also gave him the unique miracle of giving life to the dead.
Yusuf	Nabi	Allah gave him the capability to interpret dreams.
Dawud	Nabi	Allah gave him a beautiful voice; mountains and birds used to sing hymns with him, and he also knew the art of making armor using iron.
Suleiman	Nabi	Allah gave him control over Jinns, birds, and animals (the ability to understand their languages).
Muhammad	Rasool	Allah sent him to the entirety of humanity and gave him the Quran, a living miracle until the Day of Judgment.

Prophet Muhammad

- He is the last in the chain of the prophets (Rasool also).
- He was given the most challenging responsibility of delivering the universal message to all the people and nations around him.
- His message, as recorded in the Quran and Sunnah, is now preserved permanently until the Day of Judgment.
- The Quran declared that Prophet Muhammad is the **SEAL OF THE PROPHETS**.
- Muslims, in general, have been given the responsibility to spread the message of Allah to the rest of humanity (through the Quran) until the Day of Judgement.
- Allah has sent more than 124,000 prophets since the time of Adam. (Recorded in a narration attributed to Prophet Muhammad).

IMPORTANT: Prophets <u>do not</u> come to tell us how to conduct medical research, build cities, form governments, manage money and financial matters, etc. They come to guide people in their relationship with Allah, their moral behavior, and their accountability on the Day of Judgment.

The Most Merciful

- Knowledge of Allah's attributes is one of the crucial aspects that the Quran provides us with.
- Knowing the attributes of Allah helps us realize that the world we live in belongs to Him, and that we should know how to behave in it.
- They also help us build a relationship with Him when we attach ourselves to one of His attributes that we feel closer to.

And to Allah belong the best names, so invoke Him by them. (7:180)

Ar-Rahman (The Most Merciful)

- This is one of the most used attributes of Allah in the Quran. It means His mercy applies to all living and non-living creatures on Earth.
- Since the time of our creation, He has not left us without guidance at any moment. He cares about us and wants to make sure that we all become successful in the test of this life and earn Jannah.
- That is the reason He chose Prophets and Messengers among us and guided us through them.
- He provides for the one who believes in Him, as well as for the one who does not believe in Him. Even those who reject His existence are also taken care of≥
- He provides everything on Earth for us without us even asking. This is a clear demonstration of Him being the Most Merciful.

The Most Merciful taught the Quran because He had created a human being and had given him speech. (55:1-4)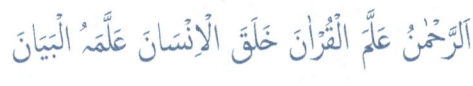

Pick a Prophet or Messenger from the Quran and write three to five unique things about him. Give a reference from the Quran (Surah and verse) where it is mentioned.

Time to Complete: _____

PROPHETS WORD SEARCH

Instructions

- Print and find the names.
- Please take a picture of the completed search and submit it via Google Classroom or show it in the class.

U	I	R	D	A	M	M	A	H	U	M	D	S	T
A	A	A	B	R	E	A	S	D	H	H	I	A	U
D	L	A	O	E	M	U	A	I	H	U	B	A	L
A	I	I	S	H	A	Q	A	U	S	D	H	N	M
E	Z	I	H	H	A	A	Y	H	A	S	A	U	E
Z	A	K	A	R	I	A	H	I	L	D	H	H	H
I	I	B	R	A	H	I	M	K	E	H	U	A	M
A	D	A	L	L	A	M	H	L	H	S	A	H	A
A	D	H	M	O	A	A	S	Y	A	A	S	I	D
S	I	Z	M	I	S	M	E	A	A	R	M	A	A
L	I	A	M	S	I	M	E	U	S	Q	I	I	A
U	T	M	E	D	D	A	R	S	M	U	O	B	I
A	A	A	I	A	S	H	D	N	U	Y	M	O	H
A	S	A	O	S	A	D	I	B	A	E	L	H	B

ADAM
HUD
SALEH
YAQOOB
IBRAHIM
ISA
IDREES
NUH
LUT
ISMAIL
MUHAMMAD
ISHAQ
ZAKARIAH

Chapter 3

A Prophet Predicted

In this chapter, we will learn the predictions about the arrival of Prophet Muhammad that are mentioned in the previous scriptures.

Prophet Ibrahim and His Family

- Prophet Ibrahim is considered the father of the prophets. The chain of the Prophets from him is shown below:

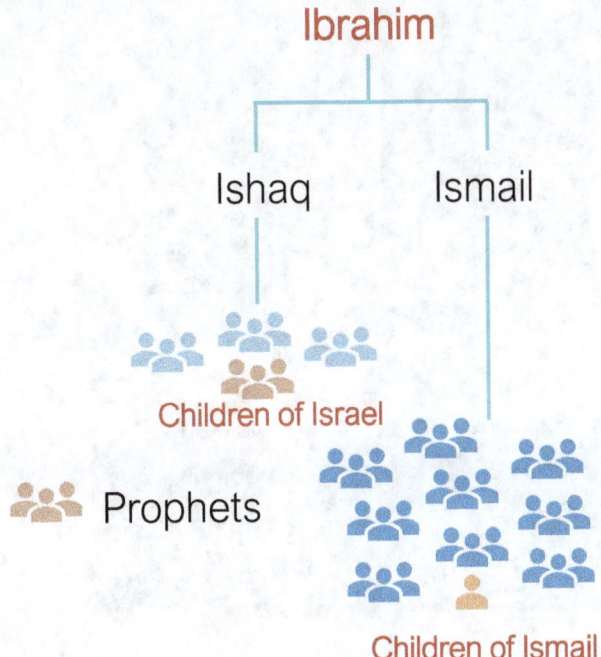

- God tested him through many difficult trials before he was honored.
- God honored Ibrahim and his next generation by giving them the responsibility of the 'leadership' of the world for preaching the message of God.
- Responsibility was to spread the message of the oneness of God to the other nations that did not get the message directly.
- His two children, Prophet Ishaq and Ismail, founded two great nations from which other prophets came.

 **Q** What tests did Prophet Ibrahim go through?

- King threw him into a fire for his beliefs.
- He was asked to 'sacrifice' his son for the sake of Allah.
- He was asked to leave his family, including a young son, in a barren land.

Two Great Nations

- God told Prophet Ibrahim to settle his young son, Prophet Ismail, in Makkah and later, his second son, Prophet Ishaq, in Palestine.

- God blessed both lands so that Ibrahim's children would flourish there.
- In a way, God made two Centers of Worship on Earth, the worship of one true God.
- Many prophets came from Prophet Ishaq's family after him, but in Prophet Ismail's family, no prophet came until Prophet Muhammad.

Sacrifice of a beloved son

- Ibrahim dreamt that he was 'sacrificing' his son, Ismail, in the way of God; he took this dream literally.
- Ibrahim asked Ismail for his opinion on this dream.
- Ismail presented himself to what Allah commanded.
- God was very pleased with their obedience and replaced Ismail with a sheep/lamb.
- **Interpretation of the dream:** God wanted Ibrahim to 'dedicate' (similar to sacrifice) Ismail to the house of God, which the father and son were to build together. Dedicating someone to one job is like sacrificing him/her.
- Muslims have been sacrificing animals on Eid al-Adha for thousands of years to honor the sacrifice that Prophet Ibrahim presented to his Lord.

Construction of the Kaaba

"The **first house** (of worship) that was set up for people is in Bakkah (old name of Makkah). It is the center of blessings and guidance for all in this world. It contains clear signs, and the spot where Ibrahim once stood." (3:96-97)

- God wanted to build a global house of worship in Makkah and dedicate Ismail for:
  - Keeping this house dedicated to the worship of God alone.
  - Maintaining it for pilgrims.
- The Quran called this ancient house of worship the 'House of Allah' (Baytullah).
- Importance of this House:
  - Billions of Muslims pray while facing this house.
  - Millions of Muslims now visit this house throughout the year, and especially for the Pilgrimage (Hajj).
  - The House of Allah, the Kaaba, is now considered the Center for Oneness of God.

Prayer of Prophet Ibrahim

- When Prophet Ibrahim and his son were building the House, they both made a supplication (dua) to God to send a Prophet from among the children of Ismail.
- Prophet Muhammad was the answer to that dua, reported in the Quran.

رَبَّنَا وَاجْعَلْنَا مُسْلِمَيْنِ لَكَ وَمِن ذُرِّيَّتِنَا أُمَّةً مُّسْلِمَةً لَّكَ وَأَرِنَا مَنَاسِكَنَا وَتُبْ عَلَيْنَا إِنَّكَ أَنتَ التَّوَّابُ الرَّحِيمُ. رَبَّنَا وَابْعَثْ فِيهِمْ رَسُولًا مِّنْهُمْ يَتْلُوا عَلَيْهِمْ آيَاتِكَ وَيُعَلِّمُهُمُ الْكِتَابَ وَالْحِكْمَةَ وَيُزَكِّيهِمْ إِنَّكَ أَنتَ الْعَزِيزُ الْحَكِيمُ. (١٢٨:٢-١٢٩)

"Lord! And make both of us obedient to You; make of our children also a community that will submit to You and teach us our rites of worship and accept our repentance. Indeed, You alone are Forgiving and Merciful. Lord! Send them a messenger from amongst them who shall read out to them Your verses and shall instruct them in the law and wisdom and shall purify them. You alone are the Mighty, the Wise One." (2:128-129)

Predictions of earlier Prophets

A Prophet Predicted by Musa

- Before his death, Prophet Musa gathered his people and asked them to make a promise to obey his last will.
- He then predicted the coming of a Prophet after him, gave them signs to recognize him, and instructed them to believe in him and follow him.

And my Lord said to me, What they say is right. I shall send a prophet, like you, from amongst their brothers, and put my speech into his mouth, and whatever I order him, he will say to them. And I will take retribution if he does not listen to what he says in my name. (Deuteronomy 19)

- The above prediction can be interpreted this way:

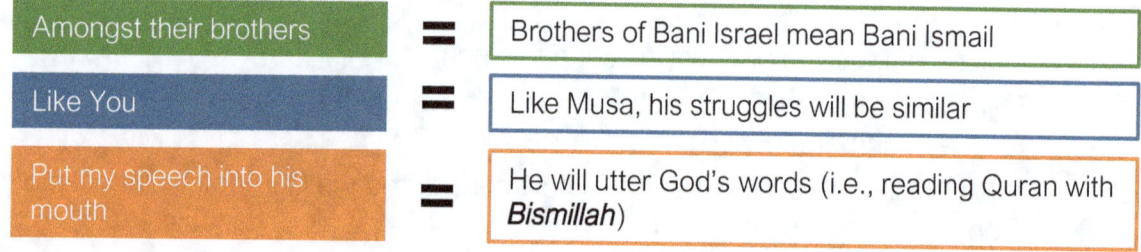

A Prophet Predicted by Daud

'The stone that the builders refused. Has become the cornerstone.
This is so because God ordained it. And it seems strange to our eyes.
This is the same day that God has set. When we shall be glad and shall celebrate, O' our Lord, save us. O' Lord, grant us a good harvest.
He who comes with the name of God is blessed. We bless you from the House of God.' (Zabur; 26:22:118).

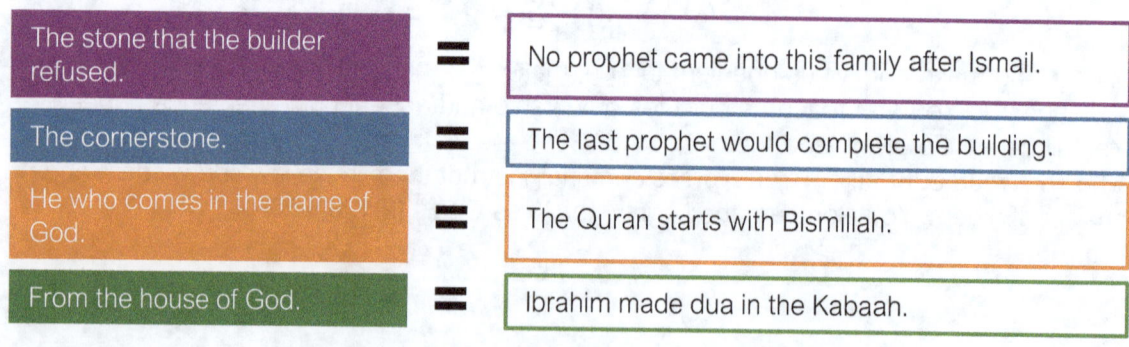

A Prophet Predicted by Jesus (Isa)

'Go to the lost sheep of the house of Israel and continue to announce that the Kingdom of Heaven is about to come.' (Matthew; 10:7-8)

- The Bible explains: The Kingdom of Heaven will be like a very small mustard seed, but when it takes root, it becomes a tall and strong tree on which birds build their nests. Or else, it is like the small amount of yeast a woman adds to the dough when making bread, causing the dough to expand and rise in a short while.

What does it mean?
- When the predicted prophet begins his mission, he will be alone, and gradually, people will join him.
- His group would grow so large that his entire nation would accept his teachings.
- With time, other nations will accept and will find peace in their hearts.
- If you look carefully, this explanation fits only Prophet Muhammad.

Do you know which three religions are called Abrahamic religions worldwide?

Shift of Religious Leadership as Predicted

- Before Prophet Muhammad, the Children of Israel were the world's religious leaders until the time of Jesus.
- After Prophet Muhammad, the responsibility of preaching the religion of God to the world until the Day of Judgment is given to the children of Prophet Ismail.
- This happened as predicted in the religious text we studied earlier.

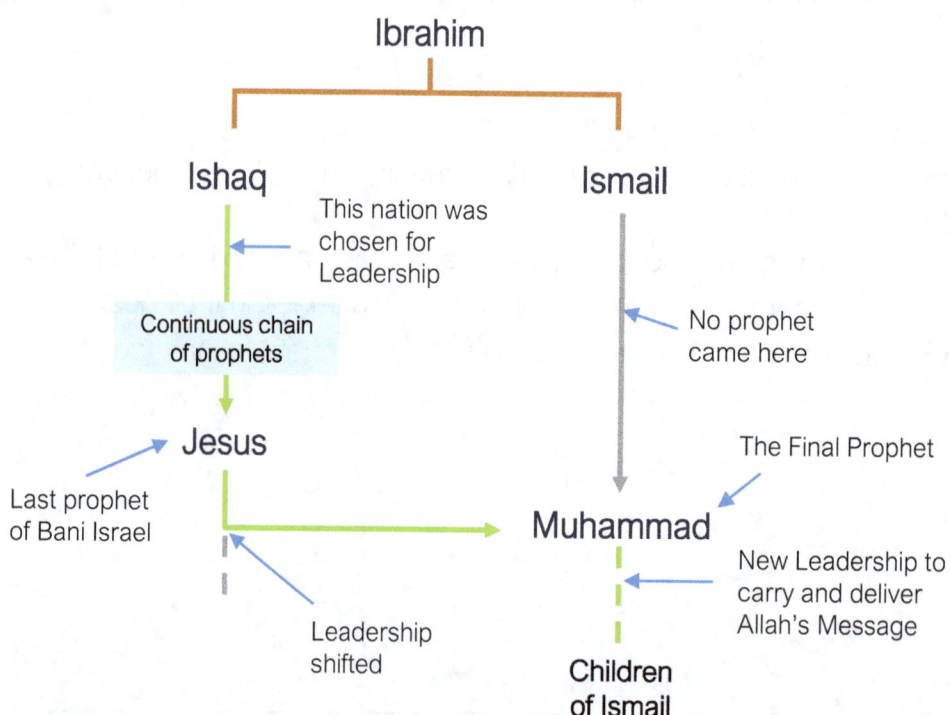

Recognizing a True Prophet

Recognizing a true prophet of God is very important. We believe in him and take the revelation given to him as a source of guidance. We obey him and seek guidance through him in many affairs of our lives. There are many signs of a true prophet, and news of his coming, as mentioned in the old scriptures, is just one of them.

The All Responsive (who accepts your requests)

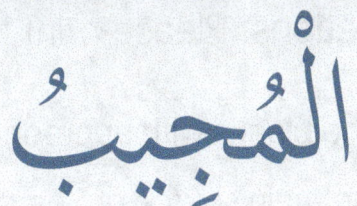

- God promised in the Quran that He answers our prayers. For some prayers, we see the results in this world in our life, and for some, we will see the results in the Hereafter.
- God responds to our prayers according to His Wisdom and Knowledge because He knows what is best for us, as He is the God of the Universe.
- But when it comes to guidance, He never rejects the dua in this life.
- God answered Prophet Ibrahim's prayer, and Prophet Muhammad was sent 4000 years after that prayer.
- Prophet Muhammad taught us to make dua for everything, but not to be hasty about the results. Making dua and then waiting for its results is part of our test.
- Making dua is a form of worship because it shows that you rely on Him.

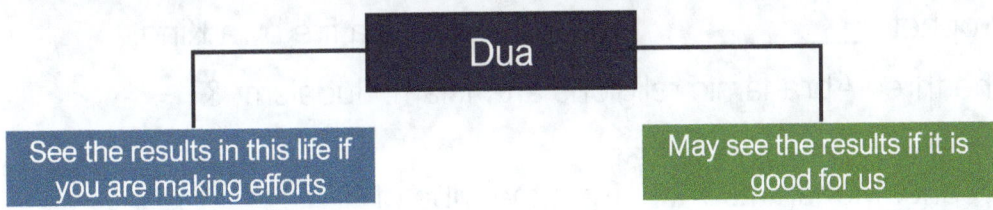

Those who are bearing difficulties for Our cause, We shall definitely guide them to Our ways [95], and undoubtedly God is with those excel in their deeds (29:69).

SEERAH ACTIVITY

Time to Complete: _____

Instructions: Please print this page and complete it.

Fill in the blanks with appropriate words:

1. The main source of Seerah is _____.
2. Studying _____ increases our love for the Prophet.
3. Prophet Muhammad is now the only source of _____ for us.
4. Prophet Muhammad was born in _____ AD.
5. We know Allah through His _____.
6. Allah wants to give us a good life in the _____.
7. Adam's story teaches us that our biggest enemy is _____.
8. Prophet Muhammad is the best _____ for us in religion.
9. The book of _____ was given to Prophet Moses.
10. The nation of Messengers is _____ if they reject him.
11. Prophet _____ was thrown into a fire by a King.
12. The three Abrahamic religions are: Islam, Judaism, & _____.
13. Prophet Muhammad was from the tribe of _____.
14. Pagans used to call angels _____ of Allah.
15. _____ is the religion of all Prophets.

Shaytan	Quraish	Ahadith	Attributes	Guidance
570	Hereafter	Daughters	Model	Islam
Torah	Ibrahim	Seerah	Christianity	Punished

Chapter 4

Condition of Arabia before the Prophet's Birth

In this chapter, we will learn the conditions of various tribes and nations in that area and around it before the birth of Prophet Muhammad

Religious Groups

- Before the birth of Prophet Muhammad, the following religious groups existed in and around Arabia:

Children of Ismail

- Prophet Ismail was married into the tribe of Banu Jurhum.
- His family took responsibility for maintaining the Kabaah.
- For a short time, this job was taken over by the tribe of Jurhum, but the pilgrims were unhappy with them, and after a few battles, the children of Ismail took over the maintenance of the Kabaah.

Idol Worshippers: Due to greed and political rivalry, some people introduced idols into the Kabaah, and people started associating them as partners with God.

Haneef: There were people among them who remained on the path of Prophet Ibrahim and Ismail. They used to be called *Haneef* (literally meaning focused on one).

Jews	Christians
- The Jews considered themselves God's chosen people and believed the leadership role was their right. - They became arrogant and repeatedly twisted God's message to suit their own interests. - Many Jewish tribes (some of them were ruling tribes) settled in the old area of Yathrib (new Medinah). - They migrated from the times of the Romans and settled there, anticipating a prophet.	- There were many Christian tribes in the area. - The mighty Byzantine Empire was ruled by the Romans, who spread Christianity to many neighboring countries. - Countries that adopted Christianity as their religion were Abyssinia, Yemen, Syria, and many Arab tribes.

Zoroastrians (Persians)

Another powerful empire neighboring Arabia was the Persian Empire, which believed in Zoroastrianism. This ancient (founded 4000 years ago) religion also believed in one God and was said to be based on the teachings of Prophet Zoroaster. They were always in fierce competition with the Byzantines.

Arab Tribes and Idol Worship

- In those days, the tribes didn't have a single king or a government building; instead, they managed everything through councils and shared responsibility.
- Each tribe had a leader, called a Raees or Shaykh, who represented the tribe in the council, where all affairs were discussed and settled.

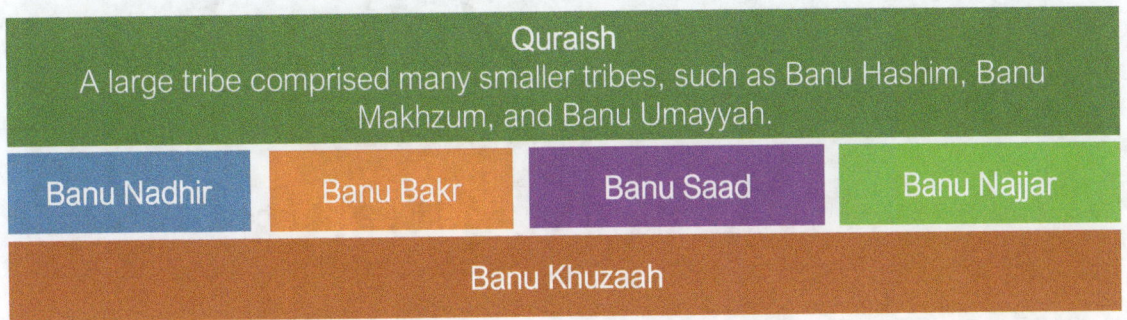

Quraish
A large tribe comprised many smaller tribes, such as Banu Hashim, Banu Makhzum, and Banu Umayyah.

Banu Nadhir	Banu Bakr	Banu Saad	Banu Najjar

Banu Khuzaah

Note: *Banu* means "Children of .."

- Once, the tribe of Banu Khuzaah took charge of maintaining the Kabaah.
- They were good in the beginning, but later lost interest in this noble work.
- Amr Bin Lahayy, one of the chiefs of Banu Khuzaah, introduced idols into the House of God.
- One time, he brought a huge statue of Hubal from Syria on his way back.
- He started putting fear of the idols in the hearts of the people, and they began praying for their blessings (good luck) on main events (like the birth of their children, etc.).
- Later, other idols entered the House of God.

The chief god of pre-Islamic Arabia was *Hubal*, with three daughter goddesses: *Laat*, *Manat,* and *Uzza.*

Why must we be careful when starting something new if we are in a leadership position?

Political Situation in the Region

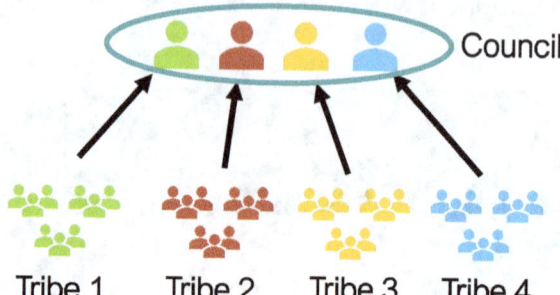

Tribal leaders would run the affairs of the area through mutual consultation

Council

Tribe 1   Tribe 2   Tribe 3   Tribe 4

- It was a typical tribal society in which chiefs of large tribes represented their tribes in collective matters.

- In those days, your family and the wider tribe were your safety net. If someone attacked you, your whole family and tribe would jump in to defend you. This made everyone feel safe because they knew their "big family" had their back.

- They had rules based on tradition and honor. Breaking a rule didn't just get you in trouble with the Shaykh; it made your whole family look bad. This encouraged everyone to be good citizens and work together.

- At that time, the leadership remained divided between two major Arab branches: the Adnanides (Emigrants) and the Qahtanides (Original Arabs).

- Prophet Ismail (Adnanides) maintained authority over Makkah as well as the maintenance of Kabaah in his lifetime (religious leadership).

- Later, this authority was transferred to Banu Jurhum.

- Due to Banu Jurhum's misbehavior, the tribe of Ismail took over again.

- Chiefs of major and powerful tribes used to meet in An-Nadwa (assembly house) for consultation and decisions.

Powerful Empires Around Arabia

- A few powerful empires had a significant influence over local tribes and smaller regions. Some of these are discussed here.

Byzantine

- Oppressive and powerful regime.
- They used to collect a lot of taxes from people.
- Elites used to take wealth from farmers for their misuse and amusement.
- Ordinary people were depressed and distressed.
- A monk-like life was widespread.
- They used to play bloody and brutal sports.

Persian/Sassanids

- Much larger and more powerful.
- A few elites of the society took all the benefits while the ordinary people were poor and in great distress.
- This resulted in many revolts; bandits and gangsters preyed upon the nobles' property.
- All civil and military powers were in the hands of the Emperors, who acted as gods.

Yemen

- The people of Sheba were among the oldest pure Arab nations in Yemen.
- The Romans conquered Yemen and even helped the Abyssinians occupy Yemen.
- Abraha, a Christian army leader, killed the ruler of Yemen, Ariat, and took rulership of this land.
- He was the one who sent an army of soldiers to demolish the Kabaah.

Abyssinia

- Under the influence, Abyssinia (now known as Ethiopia) was ruled by a king, Negus, or Al-Najashi.
- He was renowned for his justice and for protecting human rights.
- This is the land where Muslims made the first migration when they started being persecuted by the Meccans.

Religious, Moral & Economic Conditions

Religious

- Arabs believed in Allah and His attributes, but they associated other deities (in the form of idols) with Him.
- These deities were angels whom they called the "daughters of Allah".
- They believed that Allah appointed these deities.
- They polluted many worship rituals passed on to them through Prophet Ibrahim with innovations.
- For example, they used to pray but have added many innovations to their prayers.
- They were aware of fasting, but most people had abandoned it.
- They kept all the rituals of Hajj but made some changes based on their social position.

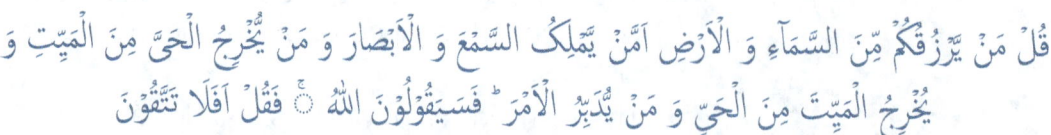

Ask them: "Who gives you food and sustenance from the skies and earth? Or, who owns your hearing and seeing? And who brings forth the living from the dead, the dead from the living. And who directs all affairs?" They will say: 'Allah. So, tell them: 'Why do you not fear Him?" (10:31)

Moral

- Wars among tribes were common and would last for years.
- People used to support their clans in matters of right and wrong blindly. That's why this period was called the "period of *Jahiliyyah*".
- Drinking and gambling were favorite pastimes.
- Support for the poor and needy was common, even in the presence of such vices.
- Interest-based trade was quite common among the Jews.
- Men would marry multiple women with no limits (some people had up to 10 to wives).
- The birth of a daughter was not welcome, and some people would bury their daughters alive due to the fear of poverty (as they could not earn anything for themselves at that time).

Economic

- They depended heavily on trade.
- Their trade journeys would take them to far-off places like Syria.
- Hajj time was the primary season for carrying out trade:
- To secure passage to pilgrims, four months, including the month of Hajj, were prohibited for fighting.

- People used to come together from faraway places for trade.
- Major trade activities used to take place at their large fairs, such as the Fair of Ukaz, Dhil-Majaz, etc.
- There was some farming and stock breeding, owned mainly by Jews.
- Economically, the Arabs were not as strong as their neighbors.

Slavery

- Slavery was a very normal part of life in Arabia and most of the ancient world.
- It was one of the largest economic institutions for the Arabs.
- Slaves (men and women) were seen more like property or "sub-humans" rather than people with rights, and their situation was often very hard.
- Slaves used to work for their masters and earn money for them.
- They had to do all sorts of hard jobs, such as working in fields, herding animals, or doing household chores.
- Slaves had very few rights. They couldn't own property, and their masters could treat them however they wanted.
- If a mother were a slave, her children were also automatically slaves, no matter who the father was.

Despite all the ills that Arab societies had, we can still see the fairness of character within the children of Ismail, who remained in charge of the House of God. They were extremely generous and charitable towards guests. They were brave and courageous, ready to sacrifice their lives for their friends. They were good at poetry and used to memorize long poems, family trees, and stories of their bravery. They were simple people, and God chose them for the qualities they possessed, to carry the torch of His Message until the Day of Judgment.

The King
The Owner

- God is the King of this world and whatever is in it.
- In this world, we have kings, but He is the King of the kings.
- He is the owner of the entire universe, whatever it has, and has supreme authority over everything.
- People receive the kingdom in this world from Him. He gives rulership to the people on Earth based on:
  - People's moral conditions.
  - His wisdom.
  - His entire scheme for this world.
- He does not change this practice as long as they deserve that position.
- He takes leadership away from people and nations when they lose the right to lead.
- We should look to Him for respect in this world and follow His guidance.

قُلِ اللّٰهُمَّ مٰلِكَ الْمُلْكِ تُؤْتِى الْمُلْكَ مَنْ تَشَآءُ وَ تَنْزِعُ الْمُلْكَ مِمَّنْ تَشَآءُ ۖ وَ تُعِزُّ مَنْ تَشَآءُ وَ تُذِلُّ مَنْ تَشَآءُ ۖ
بِيَدِكَ الْخَيْرُ ۖ إِنَّكَ عَلٰى كُلِّ شَىْءٍ قَدِيْرٌ

Pray you: "God! The Sovereign of all sovereignty, You grant sovereignty to whomsoever You please and take it away from whomsoever You please. And You grant honor to whomsoever You please and humiliate whomsoever You please. All good lies in Your control alone; Indeed, You have power over all things.

Assignment

Pick a religion and write about their concept of God, Main Personality, Place of Worship, & Practices:

Christianity   Judaism   Buddhism   Scientology

Bahai Faith   Jainism   Sikhism

Note: Let your teacher know which religion you are going to cover.

Chapter 5

Prophet's Family

In this chapter, we will learn about the tribe and family of Prophet Muhammad and his ancestors.

The Tribe of Prophet Muhammad

- Prophet Muhammad was reported to have said the following:

"God selected the Banu Kananah from the children of Ismail and the Quraysh from within the Banu Kananah. He decided to dignify the Banu Hashim from within the Quraysh and chose me from the Banu Hashim for the Prophethood." (Sahih Muslim #2276)

- In a tribal society, belonging to a noble and respected tribe was very crucial.
- God honored the tribe of Banu Hashim, who were among the Quraysh, for the birth of the Last Prophet.
- It was considered one of the most respected lineages in Arab families at that time.
- People in those times made special arrangements to preserve information about their lineage (chain of generations).

His Family Tree

The families of the father and mother merge here.

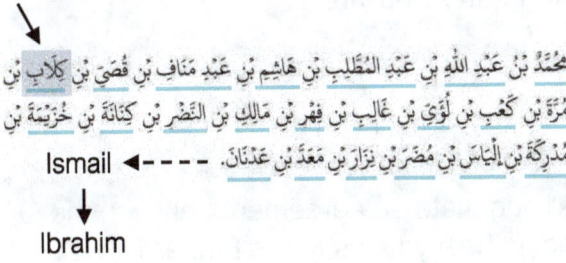

Ismail ◄---- ─ ─

Ibrahim

Prophet Ibrahim

Arabs used to memorize their family tree by heart.

- Adnan goes back to Prophet Ismail and Ibrahim.
- From **Kilab** onward, both the mother's and the father's lineages merge.

Father

Abdullah Bin Abdul Muttalib Bin Hashim Bin Abd Munaf Bin Qusay Bin Kilab Bin Murrah

Mother

Aminah Bint Wahab Bin Abd Munaf Bin Zahrah Bin Kilab Bin Murrah

Prophet's Parents & Forefathers

Abdullah Bin Abdul Muttalib

- Prophet's grandfather vowed that if God granted him ten sons, he would sacrifice one of them for the sake of God.
- When he had ten sons, he drew a lot to decide which to sacrifice. It came to Abdullah, his youngest son and father of Prophet Muhammad, every single time.
- He then approached a soothsayer to figure out what to do. She recommended slaughtering 100 camels as expiation (as a punishment) for the vow he made with God. Prophet Muhammad used to say that he was the offspring of the two who were sacrificed (Ismail and Abdullah).
- Abdullah died at a young age while on a trip with his father, Abdul Muttalib, who remained alive.

Aaminah Bint Wahab

- Aaminah bint Wahab was from the noble tribe of Bani Zuhrah within Quraysh. The tribe of Bani Zuhrah was the Prophet's maternal uncles.
- Aaminah was from Yathrib (Medinah); she was in Yathrib at the time of her marriage.
- After marriage, she moved to Makkah with Abdullah.

Hashim

- Grandfather was a very generous, honest, and kind man. He used to prepare food, especially crumbled bread in broth (hence Hashim) for pilgrims.
- He was an ambassador who helped negotiate an agreement between the Quraysh and the King of Rome, thereby avoiding heavy taxes to the Emperor.
- He died in Palestine on his way to Syria. His wife gave birth to Abdul Muttalib after his death.

Abdul Muttalib (Grandfather)

- Hashim married a woman from Banu Najjar, who put a condition on him that he stay in Yathrib. After Hashim's death, the feeding arrangements were given to his brother, Al-Muttalib.
- When Abdul Muttalib reached boyhood, his uncle, Al-Muttalib, brought him to Makkah to assume his father's role.
- He was so close to his uncle that people used to call him "the slave of Al-Muttalib, hence Abdul Muttalib".
- Banu Jurhum filled the well of Zamzam with arms and other things to close it. Abdul Muttalib saw a dream to dig Zamzam. He began serving pilgrims with Zamzam water.

Tribal associations

- The lineage (chain of generations) of Prophet Muhammad was among the most respected in Arab families, and that played a critical role in his mission.
- In tribal societies, one's influence on the people around was judged by the family to which one belonged.
- However, Islam came back to Arabia to change all that.
- The message of Islam attempted 1400 years ago to change this mentality for the very first time in the history of humanity. We are told that our tribal and family associations are merely for recognizing each other.
- Prophet Muhammad taught, through his character and the Quran, that the most honored in the sight of Allah is the one who is most God-fearing and righteous.
- In his final speech before death, Prophet Muhammad gave an important message to everyone about how to be good people and live together peacefully.
- The speech emphasizes that all humanity came from Adam and Eve and rejects superiority based on race, geography, or social status. It states that true merit is based on piety and good actions.

Why was an association with a tribe so crucial in those times?

The Creator

الْخَالِقُ

- If there could be one reason for God to ask us to worship and obey Him, it would be because He created us. A Creator has all the rights over His creations.
- God is the sole Creator of this Universe, and He created everything. He made things in such a way that they take a long time to complete and shape into their final form. There is a lot of wisdom in this form of creation. This allows us to understand how things are formed and work. This is a great blessing for us.
- He created human beings so that we are naturally inclined to form tribes, clans, societies, etc.
- The purpose of this division is to recognize each other and form a unique bond with people with whom we share family, land, skin color, or language.

يَآأَيُّهَا النَّاسُ اِنَّا خَلَقْنَكُمْ مِّنْ ذَكَرٍ وَّ اُنْثَى وَ جَعَلْنَكُمْ شُعُوْبًا وَّ قَبَآئِلَ لِتَعَارَفُوْا ۚ اِنَّ اَكْرَمَكُمْ

عِنْدَ اللهِ اَتْقَكُمْ ۚ اِنَّ اللهَ عَلِيْمٌ خَبِيْرٌ

O mankind! We have created you from a male and a female and made you into nations and tribes so you may know one another. Verily, the most honorable of you with God is the one who has piety. Verily, Allah is All-Knowing, All-Aware. (Surah Hujraat: 13)

Who created God?

- Some people ask: if God created everything, then who created God?
- The simple answer to this question is that He is an uncreated being.
- We have only seen created beings, that's why we ask this question. When we will see God in the Hereafter, we will realize that He is not made.

Chapter 6

Birth of Prophet Muhammad

In this chapter, we will learn about the events surrounding his birth and arrival in this world.

The arrival of the final Prophet

The incident of the Elephants

- Abraha was a Christian ruler of Yemen who once tried to attack the Kabaah with a large army, including elephants.
- He was upset because one of the Arabs defiled a newly built church in Yemen.
- He chose the Holy Months (Arabs were not allowed to fight) to attack because he thought the Arabs would not fight back.

https://madainproject.com/abraha

- God destroyed his plan, and he had to face the Arab tribes before entering Makkah.
- Suddenly, birds of prey descended in flocks, pelted his army with stones from the air, and later cleaned the flesh from the bodies, thus removing the bad odor of the dead.
- Some historians say that the unarmed pilgrims pelted his army with stones from the top of Mina and destroyed it, not the birds. Birds only cleaned the flesh of the dead bodies.
- This was considered an unusual event in the history of the Arabs.
- Abdul Muttalib, the Prophet's Grandfather, made a dua to God about protecting His house. He strongly believed that every man protects his home and family, and that this is the House of God; therefore, He will protect it, as He is much more powerful than Abraha's army.

The arrival of the last Prophet

- Four thousand years after Prophet Ibrahim and five hundred and fifty years after Isa (Jesus), it was time for Prophet Ibrahim's prayer to be answered.
- God sent His final Prophet to this world before He ceases this practice. This was a great moment in world history.
- Prophet Muhammad arrived, who would:
    - Be the last Prophet in the chain of Prophethood.
    - Be the Prophet for the entire humanity, not just for a nation.
    - Deliver and preserve God's message in such a manner that it would be impossible to hide any part of it or to change it.
    - Fulfill the predictions made in the previous books
    - Give the final law of God to the entire humanity until the Day of Judgment.

His Birth

The incident involving the elephants became so important in Arab history that they began their calendar from this date, and this year was called the Year of the Elephant. Prophet Muhammad was born in the same year.

- Historians agree that Prophet Muhammad was born on a Monday during the second week of Rabi Al-Awwal.
- The generally accepted date is the 12th, but research shows it would not come on a Monday if this were true.

- According to calculations by the Egyptian astronomer Mahmood Pasha, his date of birth was the 9th of Rabi Al-Awwal.
- According to the Christian Calendar, his birth date was the 22nd of April, 571 AD.

His Full Name

- Many people have multiple names, and sometimes one name becomes more popular than the other among people around you.
- **Ahmad** was the Prophet's actual name, even mentioned in previous scriptures, but Muhammad was popular. The names like Mustafa (the chosen one) were features that were used by many people later in history, attached to the name Muhammad.
- Arab people used to address a person by their first child's name as a sign of respect. It means Father of Qasim.

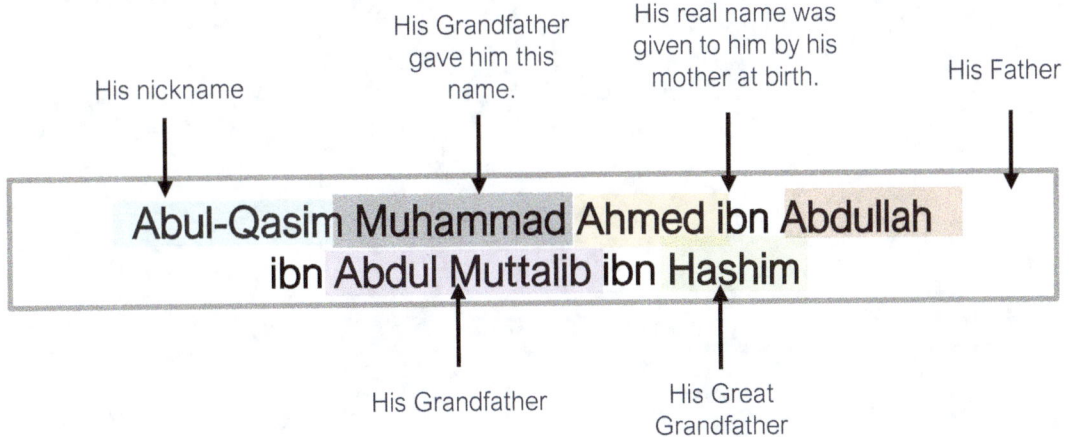

Born as an orphan

- Abdullah died before Prophet Muhammad was born.
- Orphans in tribal societies face many challenges.
- They don't have their father's support, which often results in a tough childhood.

Training for Prophethood

- The prophethood contains big responsibilities, and the prophet is given special training from birth to lay a strong foundation.
- Dealing with all types of people and situations is important for a prophet when performing the difficult job of prophethood.
- The prophet had to go through challenging times in his childhood that made him a strong person in the end.
- He was able to relate to orphans and poor people very easily.

Because Prophet Muhammad was born as an orphan and led his childhood life with no protection from his father or mother, he greatly emphasized the welfare of the orphans later as part of God's teachings. He said in a hadith: *"I and the person who looks after an orphan and provides for him, will be in Paradise like this"*, putting his index and middle fingers together **(Sahih Al-Bukhari 5659).**

The Guardian or Protector

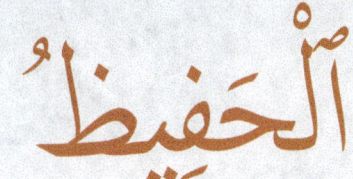

- The name of Allah, Al-Hafeez, is mentioned in the Quran, but in the Ahadith, Al-Haafiz is also mentioned.
- Allah is the guardian and protector of everything, and if He protects something or someone, no one can harm them.
- Since He created this life for a test, He sometimes allows harm to come to us.
- Kabaah is His dedicated place of worship, so He protected it from King Abraha.
- He protected the Quran for us.

إِنَّ رَبِّي عَلَى كُلِّ شَيْءٍ حَفِيظٌ

Indeed, my Lord is Guardian over everything. (11:57)

Draw a picture showing Abraha attacking Kabaah with elephants and birds attacking them. Draw with your hand and color it.

Chapter 7

Childhood and Upbringing

In this chapter, we will learn about the childhood of Prophet Muhammad, including his early upbringing in his birthplace and the nearby village.

His childhood and upbringing

- The childhood of Prophet Muhammad was not significantly different from that of other children.
- In those days, it was tradition for a child to be raised in a pure and healthy environment. To protect the child from illnesses and diseases, their parents usually keep them away from busy places, so that only a few people (i.e., one family) interact with them.

Fosterage

- Makkah was a commercial place with so many city-like activities. It also becomes crowded, especially during Hajj.
- People from different cultures and cities used to come there, affecting the purity of morals and language.
- As stated earlier, it was the custom of the nobility of Quraysh to send away their newborns to remote deserts with Bedouin tribes. They want these families to foster their children and take responsibility for the initial upbringing. They wanted their children to learn the pure Arabic language and lead a simple life.
- The Prophet was initially breastfed by his mother and Thubiyah, who was Abu Lahab's (his uncle's) slave.
- As per the custom, Aaminah tried to find a family who could foster the Prophet for a few years and provide him with the best upbringing.
- A poor lady named Halima from Banu Saad hesitantly agreed to foster the Prophet. She was aware that, since he was an orphan, she would not be compensated too well.
- It is reported that Halima's financial situation improved when the Prophet was staying with her and her family.
- She soon realized that this child had something special.

> The Prophet once said: "I speak better than all of you because I am from the Quraysh and my language is the language of Banu Saad Bin Bakr (Tabaqat al Kubra).

Mother's death

- Parents are like a roof that provides their children with security, protection, and safety. Prophet Muhammad lost it very early in his life.
- After spending a few years in the desert with Halimah Saadia, the Prophet was brought back to Makkah.
- When he was six years old, his mother took him to Yathrib to visit the grave of her husband.

- They met the Banu Najjar, who were maternal relatives of Abdul Muttalib.
- This allowed the Prophet to become familiar with Yathrib (renamed Medinah) and its surroundings.
- On the way back, Aminah fell ill and died at a place on the way called Abwa.
- Now he lost both his father and mother when he was only 6 years old.

Guardianship

- After his mother's death, his grandfather, Abdul Muttalib, took him under his kind guardianship and showered much kindness upon him.
- Whenever he would go to the Kabaah, he would ask the Prophet to sit next to him.
- At the age of eight, the Prophet lost his kind and loving grandfather, who had made his son Abu Talib, the Prophet's paternal uncle, his heir. The Prophet then came under his uncle's guardianship.
- The Prophet was always very dear to Abu Talib, right from his childhood, and remained under Abu Talib's protection.
- In those days, you must have protection from a tribe, and he remained in his protection until Abu Talib died.

Interests and activities during youth

Swordplay   Archery

- As a pastime, the Prophet used to take camels and goats out for grazing.
- In those days, slaves carried out such tasks.
- During his time with Halima Saadia, he saw young boys shepherding, for whom it was a means of earning a livelihood, not just a hobby.
- Shepherding taught him how to be a responsible person.
- Prophet Muhammad was an excellent archer, swordsman, fencer, and wrestler.

Prophet Muhammad once said that many prophets were shepherds because it taught them how to become responsible and caring.

Born and Raised as an Orphan

Born and raised as an orphan, Prophet Muhammad developed qualities that might have been lacking had he been raised in a loving home with caring parents who earned a good livelihood. The rough circumstances in his life made him stronger, more independent, more mature, and wiser very early on. He experienced poverty, the loss of blood relatives, and hardships that made him more compassionate, merciful, and, indeed, more sensitive to human suffering.

Discuss the advantages and disadvantages of village and city life. Which one do you think is better?

The Most Loving

- God is the Most Loving, and He loves His creation more than anything.
- His love for us is an active, manifest form of love that goes beyond mere emotion.
- His love is manifested through the countless blessings and bounties that He has given to His creations without asking.
- Sometimes, we see hardships in our lives, but they are there to bring out the best in us.
- He tests us through hardships to give us the permanent pleasures of Paradise.
- In difficult times, He is always ready to help us when we ask.
- Al-Wadud is the one who places affection between spouses and the love of a mother for her child.

وَ اسْتَغْفِرُوْا رَبَّكُمْ ثُمَّ تُوْبُوْٓا اِلَيْهِ ۭ اِنَّ رَبِّيْ رَحِيْمٌ وَّدُوْدٌ

And listen [if you want to remain secure,] seek forgiveness from your Lord; then turn back towards Him. In reality, my Lord is extremely Merciful and very Loving."

SEERAH ACTIVITY

THEN and NOW

Pick one topic and write a paragraph or create a chart to compare between then and now for that topic.

Topics

1. Life of a 10-year-old child (boy or girl)
2. Hobbies and passing free time
3. Food and Clothing
4. Socialization and communication
5. Travel and Transportation
6. Learning and Education

Instructions

- It is recommended to create a table with two columns and compare various aspects of the topic chosen. Use any editing tool, such as MS Word or Google Docs.

- Imagine yourself in that era and compare it with your current situation.

- You can add pictures or graphics to illustrate each point instead of writing text.

- Think about all aspects of the topic when comparing. The more the better.

- Tell us which life you would prefer.

Chapter 8

As-Sadiq Wa Al-Amin

In this chapter, we will learn about the reputation Prophet Muhammad gained early in his life before the Prophethood due to his beautiful character.

Wars in Arabia

- In the pre-Islamic era, Arab tribes fought wars over minor issues for years, and sometimes for decades.
- Since the time of Ibrahim, Arabs have considered four lunar months sacred, during which no fighting is allowed.
- Those months were: Dhul-Qadah, Dhul-Hijjah, Muharram, Rajab.
- The idea is to provide a safe passage to the pilgrims and trade caravans during this time.

Sacrilegious Wars (Harb ul Fijar)

- Prophet Muhammad was a teenager when one of the fiercest wars broke out between Quraysh and Banu Kananah on one side and the Hawazin tribe on the other.

Quraysh + Banu Kananah against Hawazin

- Sacrilegious means: to be disrespectful to something.
- The conflict was caused during the time of Ukaz, one of their largest commercial festivals, when Banu Kananah caught three men from Hawazin.
- This series of battles was important because it began during one of the sacred months when fighting was prohibited, and many people died.
- The Prophet himself attended one of these battles because of his uncles, but was mainly tasked with picking up enemy arrows.

Al-Fudoul Treaty (The Alliance of the Virtuous)

- When Banu Jurhum was in charge of the Kabaah, three people who carried the last name Fadl agreed to protect the oppressed.
- Hilf Al Fudoul means 'the alliance of many Fadl'.
- This early and vital pact was a great example of social activism, demonstrating that standing for justice was a universal human value that the tribes of Arab were well aware of, even though the rest of the world was still in the dark on these matters at the time.
- However, people forgot about the agreement over time.

- Once, a trader-pilgrim came to Makkah and did business with one of the Qurayshi lords, who refused to pay for the merchandise.
- The trader climbed onto the mount of Abu Qubays and cried for help.
- At that moment, the leaders of Quraysh, including the Prophet Muhammad's uncle Al-Zubair ibn Abd al-Muttalib, were moved to action. Representatives from several clans, including Banu Hashim, Banu Zuhra, Banu Taym, Banu Asad, and Banu Muttalib, gathered and vowed to a shared code of ethics.
- They created a new agreement on the lines of the Al Fudoul treaty to:
  - Support the needy.
  - Protect the weak against oppression.
  - Protect travelers from discrimination.

The Prophet later referred to this treaty. He is reported to have said: "I witnessed a pact of justice in the house of Abdullah ibn Jud'an that was more beloved to me than a herd of expensive red camels. If I were called to it now in the time of Islam, I would respond." (Al Tabaqaat ul Kubra)

Earning a Livelihood

Shepherding & Trade

- Initially, the Prophet worked as a shepherd, caring for other people's herds by leading them out to graze.
- He eventually began to travel for trade.
- Some narratives indicate that he used to accompany one of his uncles on many of his trade trips and that he traveled to Syria, Yemen, and Bahrain.
- His knowledge about many neighboring countries indicated that he had traveled to many countries for trade purposes before Prophethood.

The Prophet once said, "Allah did not send a prophet except that he was a shepherd." The companions asked, "And you as well?" and the Prophet replied, "Yes, I was a shepherd with a modest wage on behalf of the people of Makkah." (Sahih Al-Bukhari 2143)

- Later, he started his own trading business in partnership with others who would invest, while he provided his services for selling the goods.
- He would buy products from various traders in the city, travel with caravans to markets, sell them, and, in return, take his share of the profits.
- Many incidents are reported in the books of Seerah about these trade journeys that highlight his character and the beauty of his personality.

Discuss the qualities that a shepherd must have to do their job in the best possible manner.

The title of As-Sadiq and Al-Amin

- The Prophet gained a reputation for his judgment, honesty, truthfulness, sincerity, and trustworthiness.

- He began to be referred to as Sadiq (Truthful) and Amin (Trustworthy).

- His dealings were always managed with the greatest sense of responsibility.

- Everybody wanted to do business with him.

- When one of the companions, Saib Bin Sayfi Aiz Makhzumi, accepted Islam, people spoke of his integrity. The Prophet acknowledged that he knew that companion from the old days when he was a trader. Hearing this, the companion said: "Indeed, you always kept matters straight."

- The Quran has told us about the Prophet:

"And (O Prophet), you are on the highest standard of character" (Surah Qalam:4)

How did he earn this reputation?

- The concept of morality is tied to our relationship with family, relatives, neighbors, friends, colleagues, countrymen, tribesmen, and people from other countries.

- Our moral behavior is tested through these relationships, and when dealing with people, Prophet Muhammad passed this test with flying colors. Anyone can be good when alone.

- Lessons Learned from the Prophet's Character:
  - Honesty and good character can earn you respect in society and among people around you.
  - The good conduct of the Prophet as a shepherd and as a merchant allowed him to gain trust among the people.
  - Because he was honest, trustworthy, modest, and humble in his dealings, he was offered new opportunities and became a successful trader.

God inspired a moral compass in us

And by the soul, when We fashioned it, We inspired it with its evil and its good
(Quran 91:7-8)

وَنَفْسٍ وَمَا سَوَّاهَا
فَأَلْهَمَهَا فُجُورَهَا وَتَقْوَاهَا

- In this chapter, instead of learning one of Allah's names or attributes, we will learn a beautiful gift He gave to all humanity.
- We are moral beings. We can differentiate between right and wrong, good and evil, without any external knowledge.
- Allah created this in us right at the time of our creation.
- This ability to differentiate is the basis for all the relationships we have, whether with Allah, family, friends, neighbors, society, or the world at large.
- Ethics and morals are compatible with the nature of human beings, and that's why everybody in the world appreciates them.
- Through His Prophets and Books, God reminds us of this fact and guides us when we differ in our understanding of morality and moral behavior.
- When we value this internal gift and further nurture it as the Prophet Muhammad did, we can become a human being everyone respects and loves.
- However, the Prophet's honesty was not just a trait people would attest to; it actually earned him the official title of **as-Sadiq al-Amin (the Truthful, the Trustworthy)** among his tribesmen.
- Even when they oppressed him and rejected his message (after he became a prophet), they still trusted him with their most precious possessions. The mother of the believers, Aisha, said, "He instructed Ali to stay behind in Makkah to return all the trusts the Messenger of Allah had from the people.

Write a paragraph about one of your good qualities, how you demonstrate it in your life, and how it helps you. Share it with the class next week.

Chapter 9

His Marriage to Khadijah

In this chapter, we will learn about his first marriage to Khadijah and what role Khadijah played in his life as a Messenger.

His marriage to Khadijah

Knowing Khadjiah

- Khadijah bint Khuwaylid inherited her father's business and managed it with extraordinary skill, wisdom, and integrity.
- She was a businesswoman who sold her goods through merchants traveling to Syria and Yemen. She would take her portion of the profit from the sale.
- She once hired the services of Prophet Muhammad to take her products to the markets and sell them. The business that the Prophet managed with Khadijah's capital succeeded due to his exceptional abilities.
- He may have gone several times and done business for Khadijah.
- She had a slave named Maysarah who used to accompany the Prophet on these trips, and on one occasion, upon his return, he praised her manners, behavior, and attitude. According to various narratives, she was so pleased with what she heard that she decided to marry him.

Marriage to Khadijah

- When the Prophet was 22/23, he requested Abu Talib's daughter Umm-e-Hani Hind for marriage, but Abu Talib refused due to another proposal that came at the same time from Hubayrah Bin Abi Wahab.

- When Khadijah decided to marry him, she sent a friend, Nafisah, to ask whether he would marry her.
- He agreed. He was 25 years old.

- Khadijah's Age:
  - Khadijah was a widow and had married twice before.
  - Some historians claim she was much older than the Prophet, but others say she was slightly older (between 30 & 35), which seems right.
  - The Prophet's aunt, Safiyyah bint Abd al-Muttalib, was Khadijah's sister-in-law, having been married to her brother, Awwam bin Khawaylid, so they were already acquainted.

Khadijah and Her Role

- The Prophet had a very loving relationship with his first and only wife, Khadijah, at that time.
- Khadijah married the Prophet Muhammad because of his noble character, even though he was not as financially stable or wealthy as she was.
- This shows Khadijah's character and intelligence.

- It was part of God's plan that Khadijah married Prophet Muhammad before his prophethood for a few reasons:
- Khadijah supported the Prophet both morally and financially when he became the Prophet and embarked on a difficult mission to deliver God's message.
- After receiving the prophethood, the Prophet was asked to dedicate his time to the mission, which was only possible with Khadijah's financial support.

His love for Khadijah

- Khadijah brought three children from her previous marriage.
- She and Prophet Muhammad had six additional children from their marriage (2 sons and 4 daughters).
- Khadijah gave her slave, Zayd bin Harith, to Prophet Muhammad at the time of marriage, and the Prophet freed him and then adopted him as a son.
- Prophet Muhammad loved Khadijah so much that, even after her death, he would talk about her so much that his other wives became jealous of her.
- After her death, whenever the Prophet received gifts, money, or meat, he would send part of them to Khadija's friends and relatives, showing how much he was thinking of her.

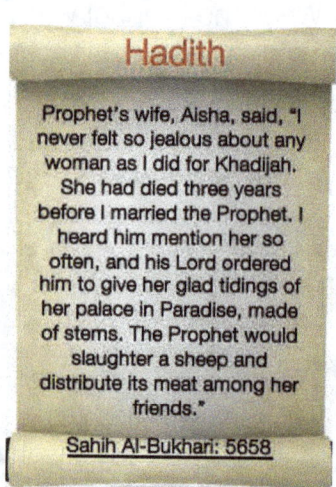

Hadith

Prophet's wife, Aisha, said, "I never felt so jealous about any woman as I did for Khadijah. She had died three years before I married the Prophet. I heard him mention her so often, and his Lord ordered him to give her glad tidings of her palace in Paradise, made of stems. The Prophet would slaughter a sheep and distribute its meat among her friends."

Sahih Al-Bukhari: 5658

His Children with Khadijah

Qasim

- He was the oldest and died at the very young age of three.
- Prophet Muhammad's nickname was **Abul-Qasim**, a practice in Arab tradition of calling the father by his eldest son's name.

Zainab

- She was the eldest daughter.
- She was among the earliest Muslims, but her husband, Abu Al-Aas, did not accept Islam. Quraish forced Abu Al-Aas to divorce her, but he refused.
- She was attacked when she was trying to migrate to Medina, which ultimately was the reason for her death after a few months.

Ruqayyah

- She was the second daughter who was first married to the son of Abu Lahab, who divorced her under the pressure of his father after she accepted Islam.
- She later married Uthman ibn Affan, a great companion and the third Caliph of the Muslims.
- They migrated twice, first to Abyssinia and then to Medina.
- She died in Medina while Muslims were fighting the Battle of Badr. Uthman was excused from the battle for this reason.

Umm Kulthoom

- She was the third daughter, who was also originally married to the son of Abu Lahab, who divorced her under the pressure of his father after she accepted Islam.
- After the death of Ruqayyah, the Prophet Muhammad married Umm Kulthum to Uthman bin Affan.
- That is the reason Uthman bin Affan was called "*Dhun-Norayn*", the one with two lights.

Fatimah

- She was the youngest daughter and most loved by Prophet Muhammad, especially after the death of her two older sisters.
- She grew up in the time when Prophet Muhammad was struggling as a result of the mission that God had assigned to him.
- She was married to Ali Ibn Talib, the cousin of Prophet Muhammad and the fourth Caliph of Muslims.
- She was the mother of the famous grandsons of Prophet Muhammad, Hasan and Hussein.
- She died six months after Prophet Muhammad left this world.

Abdullah

- He was the other son of Prophet Muhammad, younger than Qasim.
- He also died in his childhood at a very young age.

Prophet Muhammad buried all his children with his own hands in his lifetime, except Fatimah. Imagine the test that God put Prophet Muhammad through and his patience with the Will of God.

The Bestower

- The root word of Al-Wahhab is Hiba, which means gift. Allah is the Bestower of the Gifts.

- A gift is not conditional upon your efforts to get it; it is just given without asking.

- Also, Allah does not give you gifts once or twice, but all the time, but you don't realize or appreciate them.

- Spouse, children, siblings, house, car, health, education, free time… we can't count all the gifts God gives us day in and day out.

- When you lose something, stop for a moment and think of all the things that you have received compared to what you have lost; you will find no comparison.

- A gift is given to someone you remember, love, and care about.

- We may forget Allah, but God does not forget us.

- The final prophet of Allah, the man closest to Allah, lost three of his children at a very young age. He even lost some of his grandchildren during his lifetime. He grieved for his children's and grandchildren's deaths. It is okay for us to do the same. However, we must never forget Allah in our grief and refrain from saying anything that would displease Him.

- Remember, Allah is the bestower and giver because He is the owner of everything; He can take it back at any time He wants.

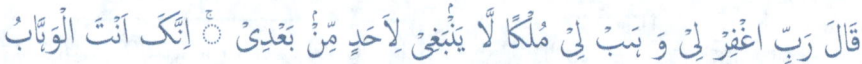

"Lord! Forgive me and bless me with a kingdom that you have not given to anyone but me. Indeed, you are the Bestower. (38:35)

What attracted Khadijah to the Prophet Muhammad for marriage? Is there a lesson for us in this amazing decision she made? She became the wife of the last Prophet of Allah on Earth.

Chapter 10

Rebuilding Kabaah

In this chapter, we will learn about the event of rebuilding Kabaah that happened before Prophet Muhammad became a Messenger.

History of Kabaah

- Before we get into the details of the event of rebuilding the Kabaah, let's look at the history of the Kabaah.
- Many Islamic traditions hold that the **Prophet Adam** built the first Kabaah as the first house of worship dedicated to the one God.
- Then Allah commanded **Prophet Ibrahim** and his son **Ismail** to raise the foundations of the House on its original site. They built it as an unroofed rectangular structure.
- Over centuries, up until the time of Prophet Muhammad, the monotheistic purpose of the Kabaah was lost as local tribes began placing idols within it. By the time it reportedly housed 360 idols.

Kabaah has been rebuilt multiple times

- The Kabaah has been rebuilt and restored several times in history. Scholars and historians report that the Kabaah has been reconstructed five to twelve times.
- The original structure built by Prophet Adam was reportedly destroyed during the Great Flood of Noah.

- In the centuries after Prophet Ibrahim, tribal groups like the *Amaleeq* and the *Banu Jurhum* are credited with various repairs.
- Major reconstructions occurred during the Umayyad and Abbasid periods.
- Sometimes it was constructed for renovation, and other times for natural disasters. It was expanded many times after the time of the Prophet Muhammad.

Depiction, historically   Today

Restoral of Kabaah during Prophet's time

Damage and rebuilding

- When the Prophet was 35 years old, heavy floods caused much damage to the Kabaah, and the Quraysh decided to rebuild it. To protect the Kabaah from floodwater, it was decided to raise the foundation and walls and install a roof.
- It was a blessed task for them, and everyone wanted to participate. It was decided that only funds from clean sources would be accepted from all contributors.
- A ship from a foreign land, loaded with construction material, got stuck on the sandy shores of Jeddah. The material from the vessel was then purchased and used to construct the Kabaah.
- On this blessed occasion, they divided the task of dismantling the existing infrastructure and erecting a new one.
- The original Kabaah had its northern wall in the shape of a half-circle, known as Hateem, and due to a shortage of funds, it remains incomplete to this day.

Dispute on placing the black stone

- During the reconstruction, it was time to reinstall the black stone in its place.
- Each tribe wanted the honor of doing so, but there was a risk of tribal dispute.
- Someone suggested that whoever from Quraysh would enter from the Banu Shaybah entrance next would be the arbitrator on this.

- The person who entered through that door was the man already titled As-Sadiq and Al-Amin, who was made the arbitrator.
- As a wise man who understood the tribal culture and the people's sentiments regarding Kabaah, Prophet Muhammad laid a blanket on the ground and placed the black stone at its center. He then asked the leaders of all the Quraysh tribes to lift the blanket from its sides, and then climbed the wall himself. When the blanket was raised, he took the stone and put it in its place himself.

There is a tradition that this stone was originally white, and the sins of the people around it turned it black. However, the significance of the black stone in Islam is purely symbolic, not anything else. When pilgrims start Tawaf, they kiss the stone or wave their hands towards it as a sign of renewing their pledge to God.

The Kabaah

- Today, the Kabaah stands as the spiritual center of Islam at the heart of the Masjid Al-Haraam in Mecca.
- Its four corners roughly align with the key directions (North, South, East, West).
- The Al-Shaibi family remains the traditional custodians of the Kabaah's key, a role they have held for centuries.
- Below are shown the main sections of the Kabaah in the picture.

Hateem

This is part of the Kabaah but has been left uncovered. Pilgrims feel a great privilege to enter it and offer optional prayers here.

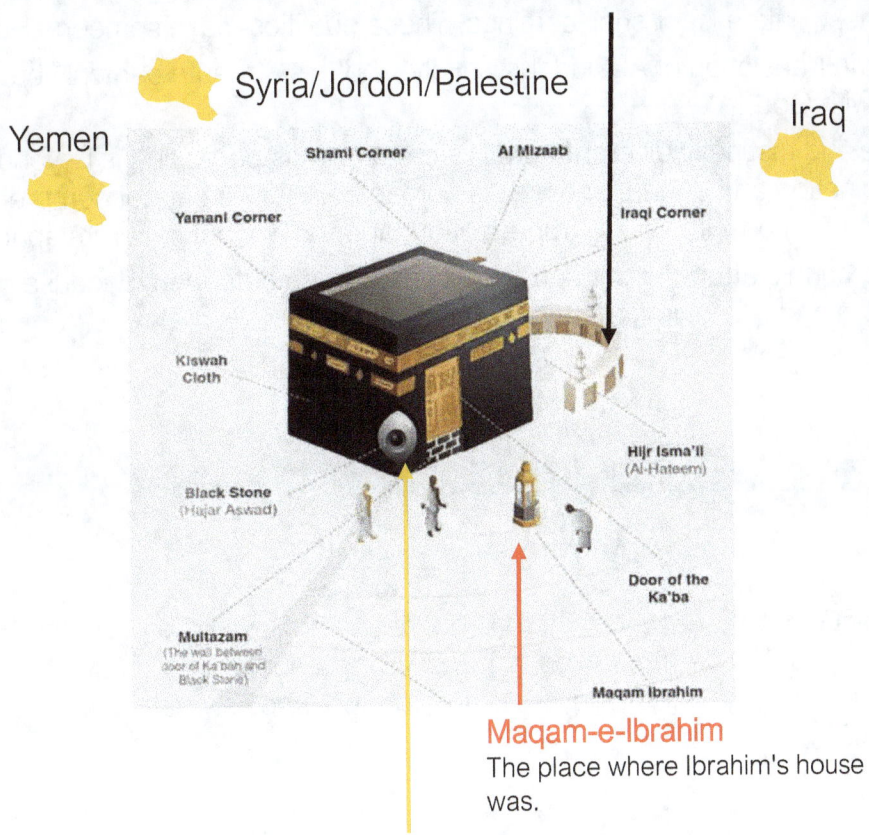

Yemen

Syria/Jordon/Palestine

Iraq

Shami Corner   Al Mizaab

Yamani Corner   Iraqi Corner

Kiswah Cloth

Black Stone (Hajar Aswad)

Hijr Isma'il (Al-Hateem)

Door of the Ka'ba

Multazam (The wall between door of Ka'bah and Black Stone)

Maqam Ibrahim

Maqam-e-Ibrahim

The place where Ibrahim's house was.

Black Stone

Pilgrims touch it or wave towards it to start each circle of Kabaah during Tawaf.

The Holy (or Pure)

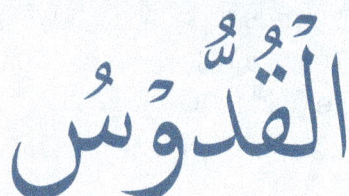

- The literal meaning of *Al-Quddus* is someone pure, far removed from imperfections, weakness, or shortcomings. These qualities make someone Holy.
- That's why the translation of Al-Quddus is Holy, and this attribute can only be associated with God.
- He is unique and distinctly different from His creation; His perfection is beyond human imagination and understanding. As human beings, we cannot comprehend how someone can be without any imperfection, and that's what sets Him apart.
- By reflecting on this attribute, our sense of worship should deepen, because only someone pure and free of imperfections deserves it.

هُوَ اللهُ الَّذِى لَا اِلٰهَ اِلَّا هُوَ ۚ اَلْمَلِكُ الْقُدُّوسُ السَّلٰمُ الْمُؤْمِنُ الْمُهَيْمِنُ الْعَزِيْزُ الْجَبَّارُ الْمُتَكَبِّرُ ۚ سُبْحٰنَ اللهِ عَمَّا يُشْرِكُوْنَ

He is the very God besides whom there is no deity, the Sovereign Lord, the Holy, the Embodiment of Peace, the Giver of Tranquility, the Guardian, the Mighty, the Extremely Powerful, the Most High; exalted is God above what they state as partners! (59:23)

SEERAH ACTIVITY

KABAAH ALBUM

Create a digital album documenting the history of the Kabaah and its various phases of construction over time through pictures and a brief description

Instructions

- Use any digital platform, such as Canva or Google Slides, to create the Album.

- Ensure that an acknowledgment or reference is included for copyrighted material.

- Add key information related to the picture, accompanied by a brief description.

- The number of photos in the album should be between 5 and 8.

Chapter 11

Responsibility of Prophethood

In this chapter, we will learn about the events related to the responsibility of Prophethood given to Prophet Muhammad and how Prophet Muhammad received it.

Makkan Phase
of Prophethood
(first 13 years)

The grave responsibility of Prophethood

- Prophethood is a God-given mission and a sacred duty entrusted to specific people to serve as the important link between God and humanity.
- Prophethood is the most difficult job one can get because it involves both intense moral and psychological pressure and severe social opposition.
- God grants prophethood according to His infinite Wisdom.

- The Prophets are unaware of this huge responsibility until the last moment.
- However, God provides a prophet with training and special support even before the Prophethood is bestowed upon him.
- Later, God makes extraordinary arrangements to help the prophet overcome complex challenges.
- The status of prophethood cannot be acquired (cannot be learned or obtained after doing hard work), because only God chooses a Prophet.

Preparation

- A prophet is assigned to deliver the following Message to the people in very clear terms:
    - Recognizing one true God.
    - Their duties toward God.
    - Their duties towards other human beings.
    - Hold firmly to God's instructions and the reward they will get.
    - To warn his people of punishment if they do not listen to God's instructions.
- God prepares such people from birth to deliver this message in the best possible way. However, they are usually not aware that God is preparing them for a mission.
- The Prophets are trained for challenging situations where they must deal with all types of people, including friends and foes (message draws enemies).
- They lead a righteous life even before the Prophethood is bestowed upon them, and they earn the people's trust early on.
- Let's look at a few examples of how God prepared two of the Prophets.

Training in life situations – Examples

Prophet Musa

- Musa had to face the most brutal tyrant of the time, the famous Pharaoh of the time.
- At the time of his birth, the Pharaoh had ordered all newborn males of the Children of Bani Israel to be killed.
- When Musa was born, God put the idea in his mother's mind to place her newborn in a basket and throw it in the river.
- It was Pharaoh's wife who adopted him as their son, and he grew up in the very palace he would later fight against.
- Throughout his early life, he had lived with the fact that the Pharaoh had enslaved his entire nation.
- He grew up to be a caring person who would not tolerate any injustice.
- One time, he accidentally killed a Coptic Christian (while trying to solve a fight) and had to run for his life as the Pharaoh wanted to capture and kill him (just because he was from the enslaved nation).
- In the city he escaped to, he had to serve his father-in-law for 10 years as payback for the dowry for his marriage.

Prophet Yusuf

- He was subjected to ill-treatment by his half-brothers. They threw him in a well and left him there to die.
- He was taken as a slave and sold in Egypt as a young boy.
- Bought by a minister, he was raised in the palace and learned many skills in governance and the management of political affairs.
- He was tested by the same women who raised him and finally thrown in jail for refusing to comply.
- He was given the authority and responsibility to manage the estate's financial matters.
- He faced his brothers in a situation where he could have taken revenge, but he did not.

Discuss some of the life situations that helped Prophet Muhammad in his prophethood later in his life.

Prophethood

Religious Beliefs

- The prophets know their people very well: their beliefs, their objects of worship and love, their feelings, their moral strengths and weaknesses.
- For example, Prophet Shoaib was a trader and knew his people's wrongdoings and their underhanded tricks. Prophet Ibrahim was well aware of the extent of the respect and love his people had for idols/statues, as he was born in a house that made them.
- Most people in the society where Prophet Muhammad was born were Polytheists (Mushrik). Only a small group of people still followed the faith of Prophet Ibrahim/Ismail and maintained a hatred for Polytheism (called Hanif).
- This group used to consider the Kabaah as the center of their worship and tried to follow as many traditions as possible from their forefathers, Ibrahim/Ismail.
- These people were honest, with high moral values, and always ready to support the good.
- Prophet Muhammad was also a Hanif and never participated in the polytheistic customs and immoral activities of other people.

Search for the Truth

- The first source of guidance on right and wrong for a human being is within a person (their nature).

- Prophets are pure human beings, and they are blessed with the natural quality of always doing the right thing.
- Some core beliefs are already inside of us:
  - There is only one God who created everything.
  - The difference between good and evil.
  - One should be held accountable for his/her actions.
- Despite living in a polytheistic culture, Prophet Muhammad knew that polytheism was wrong, but the teachings of Ibrahim and Ismail were all polluted.
- He used to practice whatever religious practices were left from the time of the Prophet Ismail in the best possible manner. He was always seeking the truth about worshiping God.
- It is reported that the Hanif people used to lean against the wall of the Kabaah and pray to God like this: *"Our Lord, we do not know how to worship You correctly: if we did, we would have done so accordingly."*

Worship at night and true dreams

- Prophet Muhammad used to practice the traditions of Prophet Ibrahim (some of which were forgotten), such as Salah, Fasting, etc.
- Before Islam, he used to spend the last 10 days of Ramadan, and sometimes more, in the cave of Hira, pondering on creation and life.
- Sometimes he would go with his family, and they would perform acts of charity (such as feeding the poor) on these occasions.

Traditions of Prophet Ibrahim

Hajj

Sacrifice

Salah

Fasting

- In the last few months before he received the revelation, he liked to be alone to worship God.
- God was preparing him and purifying his heart for receiving the revelation.
- As part of their preparation, Prophets undergo unique experiences that would be considered strange by ordinary men.
- He also started having dreams of good news that seemed as clear as daylight (meaning they came true the next day).

Angel Jibrael and his role

- God has chosen Archangel Jibrael (Gabriel) as the Messenger angel from among the angels to bring God's messages and revelation to human beings.
- Angel Jibrael has been delivering this message since his creation.

- Devils/Jinns always try to interfere with God's message. To deal with the devils, God has made Angel Jibrael extremely powerful. It has been reported in Ahadith that his wings can fill the entire horizon.
- Some other angels have different responsibilities.

Jibrael (Gabriel)

Mikaeel (Michael) (for providence like rain)

Israfeel (Angel who will blow in the horn)

Malik (Angel of Hell)

Azrael (Angel of death)

Famous Incident of Cave Hira

- The most famous incident reported about the first revelation happened in the Cave of Hira.
- It is reported that one night, angel Jibrael appeared and asked the Prophet to "read". The Prophet responded, "I cannot read." Angel Jibrael embraced him, released him, and asked again. This happened three times; finally, the Angel Jibrael read these verses and disappeared:

"Read, in the name of your Lord, Who created man from a clot of blood. Read and your Lord is highly Merciful." **(Surah Alaq:1-3)**

- Prophet Muhammad got afraid, ran to his wife, and told her about the incident.
- His wife, Khadijah, comforted him and told him that it must be something good for him because "you help the poor and the orphans, keep good relations with your kith and kin, and serve your guests generously, so God will never disgrace or dishonor you".
- Most historians concluded as a result of this incident that Surah Alaq Verses 1-3 were the first revelation.

Surah Fatihah as the first Surah (another opinion)

- Because of the topic of Surah Alaq and other reports, some historians suggest Surah Al-Fatiha was the first Surah revealed, not Surah Alaq, for the following reasons:
  - Prophet Muhammad did not report this incident directly to anyone, despite this being the most important event of his life.
  - In this incident, God never told the Prophet that he had been made a Prophet, and the Quranic verses cannot be given to someone who is not yet a Prophet.
  - The Prophet neither started preaching nor claimed prophethood after this incident.
  - The Prophets are always clear when they are given responsibility. After this incident, he became quite anxious and asked others about its reality.

The nature of the incident of the Cave of Hira suggests that it may have been revealed in a dream to prepare the Prophet, and these verses were actually revealed to him later.

The Miraculous Quran

Choice of an unlettered prophet

- Some Christian scholars and scholars of other religions argue that Prophet Muhammad authored the Quran and made it up to gain power over the People of the Book at that time. The disbelievers at the time of the Prophet Muhammad also made this claim, as documented in the Quran. It can also be said from the Quran that this was the objection of other nations when their prophets were given revelations.

- It is a historical fact that the life of the Prophet Muhammad before his prophethood shows no sign that he was engaged in reading or writing.

- The people of the book at that time used to call Quraysh the *Ummi* (people without a scripture) and considered themselves superior to them.

- Prophet Muhammad never wrote a single line or said a single word in the first 40 years of his life that could be considered writing (like an author).

- The content of the Quran is as relevant today as it was 1,440+ years ago. This cannot be true for human writing.

- There is no contradiction in the Quran, even though it was written over a period of 23 years.

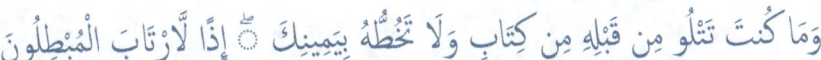

وَمَا كُنتَ تَتْلُو مِن قَبْلِهِ مِن كِتَابٍ وَلَا تَخُطُّهُ بِيَمِينِكَ ۖ إِذًا لَّارْتَابَ الْمُبْطِلُونَ

Neither did you (O Muhammad) read any book before it (this Quran), nor did you write any book (whatsoever) with your right hand. In that case, indeed, the followers of falsehood might have doubted. (Surah Ankabot:48)

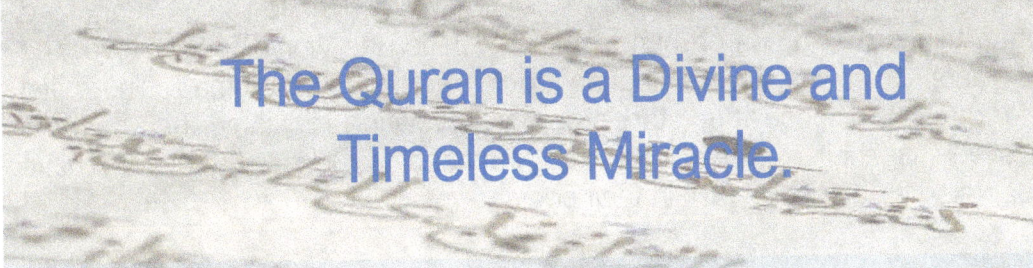

The Quran is a Divine and Timeless Miracle.

God wanted to make the Quran a living miracle.

Quran is the Guidance for mankind

- The purpose of divine religious books is to judge between right and wrong, so that people can settle their differences by understanding spiritual teachings.
- The protection of the Divine Book requires God's involvement; otherwise, it is lost over time.
- Matters of faith, such as belief in God and the Hereafter, are mostly corrupted over time, and religious books correct them.

اهْدِنَا الصِّرَاطَ الْمُسْتَقِيمَ
"Ihdina-s-sirāta-l-mustaqim"
"Guide us to the straight path"

Quran is the last book of God, not the first

- The Quran is the only original, authentic, unmodified Book of God on earth.
- God protected it, and it is still available in its original text and language, with no additions made.
- It is the ONLY source of God's guidance on religious and moral matters until the Day of Judgment.

IMPORTANT

Prophethood is a significant responsibility and a unique experience that most humans do not undergo or find easy to comprehend. Just before Prophet Muhammad was given prophethood, God enabled him to see, hear, and experience things that prepared him for the revelation he would receive over the next 23 years. This was the training period for Prophet Muhammad. The initial period is tough. Still, once they start receiving revelation regularly, they become fully satisfied that their experience is directly related to God and that they have been appointed for a specific task in their society.

The Most Generous

- The word "Kareem" encompasses all kinds of good, honor, and virtues.
- Allah is Al-Kareem because He exceeds the limits when He gives, and He is not concerned with how much He provides or to whom He gives.
- When He created us, He not only provided for us in this life without asking, but also ensured that we are constantly guided and aware of Allah's teachings so we can succeed in the Hereafter.
- The guidance necessary to earn Allah's pleasure is the greatest blessing; otherwise, we will be wandering in the dark. It is only a generous God who can send guidance in the form of the Quran.
- Because the Quran is full of benefits, blessings, and virtues, it is also called the Quran Al-Kareem.

وَ مَن شَكَرَ فَإِنَّمَا يَشْكُرُ لِنَفْسِهِ ۚ وَ مَن كَفَرَ فَإِنَّ رَبِّي غَنِيٌّ كَرِيمٌ

He who expresses gratitude does it for his own benefit, and he who shows ingratitude, then this too is his own loss because my Lord is Self-Sufficient and He is very Generous." (27:40)

Why does God protect a prophet before or after prophethood from falling into sins or errors?

Chapter 12

The Message

In this chapter, we will briefly discuss the message that every Prophet or Messenger brings, and that's what Prophet Muhammad taught when his nation changed the teachings of Prophet Ibrahim.

Bringing the True Message of Islam

- The main purpose of the prophethood of the Prophet Muhammad was to revive the central message of Islam, namely the unity of God: "There is none worthy of worship but Allah." This is called Monotheism. Other concepts of religion also become the focus, centered around this message.

There is none worthy of worship but Allah

- This core message of Islam is now saved in the Quran for all of humanity until the day of judgment.

وَ لَقَدْ بَعَثْنَا فِيْ كُلِّ أُمَّةٍ رَّسُوْلًا أَنِ اعْبُدُوا اللهَ وَ اجْتَنِبُوا الطَّاغُوْتَ

And We raised a messenger in each nation with the message: "Worship God and stay away from *at-Taghut* (Satan)." (Nahl:36)

- God specifically mentioned to stay away from Satan because he promised that he would misguide people through polytheism (*Shirk*).

Why did Satan promise Allah to misguide people through *Shirk*?

Monotheism – Belief in one True God

- Pure monotheism (oneness of God, Tawheed) means the following:
  - God is the only Creator and Maintainer of this world, and everything else is His creation.
  - NO ONE is from the nature of God (like God).
  - Only He created everything, and only He runs this world.
- Quraysh used to believe in God as the Creator of this universe, but they also associated other creatures, such as angels, with God, believing they could help them with Divine Matters. They used to worship them instead of Allah. This concept is completely against pure monotheism.
- The Quran used the word Shirk (Polytheism) for this concept and completely rejected it.
- Shirk is considered a serious crime against God because He never commanded it. So, people must invent a lie against Him to prove their partners.
- The Quran left no doubt in any sense about the unity of God.

قُلْ هُوَ اللَّهُ أَحَدٌ ۞ اَللهُ الصَّمَدُ ۞ لَمْ يَلِدْ وَلَمْ يُولَدْ ۞ وَلَمْ يَكُن لَّهُ كُفُوًا أَحَدٌ

Say [O Prophet!]: God is alone. He is the refuge for everyone. He is no one's father nor anyone's son; and there is none like Him (He is unique). (Samad:1-4)

Other deities are self-made

- The false gods people worship are usually made in the form of statues and images (fetishes).
- These statues are often made in the form of human beings or other creatures, such as angels.
- God Himself never said that any person/creature was His partner.
- That's why God called Polytheism, especially in the form of idolatry, "a lie" in the Quran, since there is no evidence for it.
- Idolatry is not limited to the worship of physical statues. There are also other idols that people submit to in their worship, such as wishes and vain desires.
- So, if God told us to do something but we 'wish' to do something else, then, in a way, we have turned our wishes into gods.

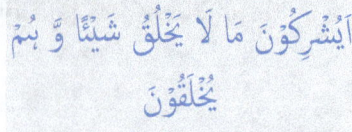

Do they ascribe to Him as partners, things that cannot create anything but are themselves created? (Aaraf:191)

Death and rebirth

- The people at the time of Prophet Muhammad used to believe in death, but they denied life after death and the Day of Judgment.

- Their main argument was that, once our bodies disintegrate into dust, how could we be brought back?

- Resurrection or rebirth (the coming back to life after death) is the starting point of the Day of Judgment and accountability.

- The Quran corrected this concept and explained that the God who created us the very first time is powerful enough to make us again.

الْمَوْتِ كُلُّ نَفْسٍ ذَائِقَةُ

Every soul shall taste death
(Aal-e-Imran: 185)

ءَإِذَا مِتْنَا وَ كُنَّا تُرَابًا ۖ ذَٰلِكَ رَجْعٌ بَعِيدٌ

(They say) When we are dead and become dust (will we return to life)? That is a distant return. (Surah Qaf:3)

Day of Judgment

- Belief in the Hereafter is the second most important concept in Islam. It is also the central message that the prophets brought.

- Like the resurrection, the people of Prophet Muhammad did not believe in the Day of Judgment or any life in the Hereafter.

- They used to mock such concepts in front of the believers, as the Quran records in many places.

- The Quran tells us that without the concept of the Day of Judgment, there is no purpose to this life. Without this, good and evil will be equal, and no one likes this.

فَوَرَبِّ السَّمَآءِ وَ الْأَرْضِ إِنَّهُ لَحَقٌّ مِّثْلَ مَا أَنَّكُمْ تَنطِقُونَ

Thus, I swear by the Lord of the Heavens and the Earth that this (the day of judgment) shall definitely come (with the same ease) as you speak.
(Dhariat: 23)

Deeds and Accountability

- In reality, the nation of Prophet Muhammad sought to avoid accountability for their deeds. These concepts are all linked.

- Accountability before God fosters self-accountability, establishing a self-check mechanism that compels people to do good to others and avoid evil.

- We create the court of law for the same purpose, and the Quran tells us that a final court of justice will be established to serve real justice.

فَمَنْ يَّعْمَلْ مِثْقَالَ ذَرَّةٍ خَيْرًا يَّرَهٗ

وَ مَنْ يَّعْمَلْ مِثْقَالَ ذَرَّةٍ شَرًّا يَّرَهٗ

So, whoever has done good, no matter how small, will see it (on that day), and whoever has done bad, no matter how small, will see it. (Zilzaal: 7-8)

أَرَءَيْتَ الَّذِيْ يُكَذِّبُ بِالدِّيْنِ ۚ فَذٰلِكَ الَّذِيْ يَدُعُّ الْيَتِيْمَ

وَ لَا يَحُضُّ عَلٰى طَعَامِ الْمِسْكِيْنِ

Did you see the person who denies the day of accountability? He is the one who repels the orphans and does not encourage people to feed the needy (Surah Maun:1-3)

Same Message

- The Quran is clear that all the prophets of God were sent to deliver the same central message of Islam. Prophet Muhammad is the last in the chain of the prophets. The core message of monotheism, the day of judgment, life in the hereafter, and accountability remained the same.

شَرَعَ لَكُمْ مِّنَ الدِّيْنِ مَا وَصّٰى بِهٖ نُوْحًا وَّ الَّذِيْٓ أَوْحَيْنَآ إِلَيْكَ وَ مَا وَصَّيْنَا بِهٖٓ إِبْرٰهِيْمَ وَ مُوْسٰى وَ عِيْسٰٓى أَنْ أَقِيْمُوا الدِّيْنَ وَ لَا تَتَفَرَّقُوْا فِيْهِ

He (God) has enjoined on you (O Prophet) the same religion which He enjoined on Noah, and which We have now revealed to you, which We enjoined on Abraham, Moses, and Jesus, with the assertion: "Adhere to this religion [in your lives] and do not create any divisions in it." (Surah Shura:13)

What kind of life would you live if you came to know that there is no Day of Judgment and no accountability? Take examples from your daily lives.

The ONE

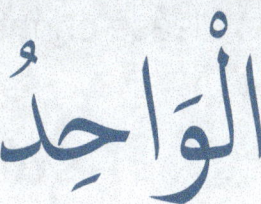

الْوَاحِدُ

- This name defines true monotheism, which means He is the one who has ever been and will always be UNIQUE and ALONE.

- He has no second. He does not depend on anyone. He neither begets anyone, nor is He begotten from any.

- The unity of God is emphasized so much in the Quran and Islam that we prefer to do things in odd numbers (adding one more count at the end to make things odd), like finishing our daily prayers with 3 Witr (2+1), counting Subhan Allah and other Adhkar odd number of times (32+1), doing Tawaf around Kabaah odd number of times (6+1), etc.

- Our daily religious acts should constantly remind us that God is alone and unique, with no partners.

وَ اِلٰهُكُمْ اِلٰهٌ وَّاحِدٌ ۚ لَآ اِلٰهَ اِلَّا هُوَ الرَّحْمٰنُ الرَّحِيْمُ

[Believers! You should now fully understand that] Your God is **one God**. There is no deity but Him. He is profoundly compassionate; His mercy is eternal. (2:163)

Time to Complete: _____

Instructions: Please print this page and complete it.

WORD MATCH

Write the most suitable word or letter in front of each statement.

1. Every living being will face this.
2. Associating partners with Allah.
3. Worshipping one God, Allah.
4. The day when people will see the results of their deeds.
5. Worshipping man-made idols.
6. Only this will help on the Day of Judgment.
7. This Surah teaches us Tawheed.
8. This means coming back to life after death.
9. This is the second most important belief in Islam.
10. Prophet Muhammad was from this tribe.

A. Quraish   B. Resurrection   C. Hereafter   D. Death

E. Monotheism   F. Good Deeds   G. Shirk   H. As-Samad

I. Idolatry   J. Day of Judgment

Chapter 13

Delivering the Message

In this chapter, we will see how God informed the Prophet about his Prophethood and asked him to start preaching the message. At the same time, we will learn Quraish's initial reaction.

Incident of First Revelation

Prophet's meeting with Jibrael

- The Quran itself records the incident of the first revelation and Jibrael's meeting with the Prophet. The implication is that he appeared to the Prophet and was seen with his eyes open.

- The incident is recorded in Surah Najm.

- This is a mention of great affection with which Jibrael taught the Prophet, so that whatever guidance he was given was fully heard and was understood by him.

- Prophet Muhammad saw Angel Jibrael twice in his original form. In one of these incidents, he was informed that he is now a Prophet of God. The Quran stated that he did not get worried in any of these incidents, unlike in the incident of the Cave of Hira.

وَ النَّجْمِ إِذَا هَوٰى مَا ضَلَّ صَاحِبُكُمْ وَ مَا غَوٰى وَ مَا يَنْطِقُ عَنِ الْهَوٰى اِنْ هُوَ اِلَّا وَحْيٌ يُّوْحٰى عَلَّمَهٗ شَدِيْدُ الْقُوٰى

ذُوْ مِرَّةٍ ۪ فَاسْتَوٰى وَ هُوَ بِالْاُفُقِ الْاَعْلٰى ثُمَّ دَنَا فَتَدَلّٰى فَكَانَ قَابَ قَوْسَيْنِ اَوْ اَدْنٰى فَاَوْحٰى اِلٰى عَبْدِهٖ مَآ اَوْحٰى

مَا كَذَبَ الْفُؤَادُ مَا رَاٰى اَفَتُمٰرُوْنَهٗ عَلٰى مَا يَرٰى وَ لَقَدْ رَاٰهُ نَزْلَةً اُخْرٰى عِنْدَ سِدْرَةِ الْمُنْتَهٰى عِنْدَهَا جَنَّةُ الْمَاْوٰى

اِذْ يَغْشَى السِّدْرَةَ مَا يَغْشٰى مَا زَاغَ الْبَصَرُ وَ مَا طَغٰى لَقَدْ رَاٰى مِنْ اٰيٰتِ رَبِّهِ الْكُبْرٰى

By the star when it sets. Your companion (the prophet) has neither gone astray nor erred. Nor does he speak of his desire. It is only a revelation that is inspired. He was taught by one mighty man in power (angel Jibrael), who had a great character when he appeared while he was on the highest part of the horizon. Then he approached and came closer and was at a distance of two bows' length or (even) nearer; so did (Allah) convey the revelation to His slave (the prophet). The prophet's heart did not deny what he saw. Will you then dispute with him about what he saw? And indeed, he saw him (angel Jibrael) another time in a descending state near Sidrat ul Muntaha. Near it is the Paradise of Abode, when that covered the lote tree, which did cover it! His sight did not turn aside, nor did it transgress the limits. Indeed, he did see the Greatest Signs of his Lord. (Surah Najm: 1-18)

Revelation started in Ramadan

- Regardless of which verses were first, the two verses in the Quran indicate that the first revelation occurred in the month of Ramadan.

- In Surah Qadr, God said He revealed this Quran in the night of power – Lailatul Qadr.

- In Surah Dukhan, God said that He had designated this night of power for deciding the most significant matters regarding the world, and the revelation of the Quran is one of them.

- God also explained in Surah Jinn that He made special arrangements for the protection of the Quran as it came down from the sky through the Angel Jibrael.

- He had set up barriers against the entry of devils, including Jinns, who could listen in on the revelation on the way and interfere in its delivery to Prophet Muhammad.

What is revelation (Wahi)?

- The exact nature of revelation is unknown to us because our only sources of knowledge in this matter are God and the Quran.

- It is a matter between God and His messenger, and human beings are not given any more knowledge about it than God intended.

- Wahi, or revelation, is how God communicates with His prophets. Prophet Muhammad has shared some of his experiences, but his companions can only observe them from the outside.

- Prophet's wife, Ayesha, reported that the Prophet Muhammad said about the nature of revelation. "Sometimes it is like the ringing of a bell; this form of revelation is the hardest of all, and then this state passes off after I have taken what is revealed to me. Sometimes, the Angel comes as a man and talks to me, and I take whatever he says." Aisha reported on a freezing day that she noticed sweat dripping from the Prophet's forehead (after it was over).

- Conclusion: Our knowledge of Wahi is minimal.

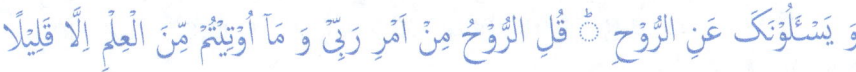

And they ask you about the reality of revelation (Wahi), tell them it's a command from God, and you have not been given any knowledge about it, but a little
(Surah Israa: 85)

The beginning of preaching

- The first of the two events (on the previous slide) was used to give prophethood to Prophet Muhammad (i.e., he was told that he was now a prophet and what his responsibilities would be).
- It is reported that Surah Fatiha (the first Surah) was the first complete Surah revealed to Prophet Muhammad.
- Surah Fatiha is a dua, and its relationship with the rest of the Quran is the answer to that dua.
- In another narration, the Prophet said that the initial verses of Surah Muddathir were revealed as the first instructions for beginning to deliver the message.
- The Prophet was asked to call people towards divine guidance and, if they rejected it, to warn them of dire consequences in the form of punishment in this world and the Hereafter.
- There is a difference of opinion among historians over which Verses/Surahs were the first to be revealed. The majority of historians say that the verses of Surah Alaq may be the first, but the instructions for preaching came later. This is a matter of historical debate, and scholars differ on such issues.
- It is reported that there was a gap between the two sightings of Angel Jibrael. The purpose was to give Prophet Muhammad time to prepare himself for a mighty task with God's help.

اَلْحَمْدُ لِلّٰهِ رَبِّ الْعٰلَمِيْنَ ۙ الرَّحْمٰنِ الرَّحِيْمِ ۙ مٰلِكِ يَوْمِ الدِّيْنِ ۚ اِيَّاكَ نَعْبُدُ وَ اِيَّاكَ نَسْتَعِيْنُ اِهْدِ نَا الصِّرَاطَ الْمُسْتَقِيْمَ ۙ صِرَاطَ الَّذِيْنَ اَنْعَمْتَ عَلَيْهِمْ ۙ غَيْرِ الْمَغْضُوْبِ عَلَيْهِمْ وَ لَا الضَّآلِّيْنَ

All Praises and Thanks belong to Allah, the Lord of the Universes. The Most Merciful, the Always-Merciful. The owner of the Day of Judgment. We worship you alone and seek help from you alone. Guide us to the straight path, the path of those whom you have blessed and not of those who received your anger and those who are misguided (Surah Fatiha)

يٰٓاَيُّهَا الْمُدَّثِّرُ ۙ قُمْ فَاَنْذِرْ ۙ وَ رَبَّكَ فَكَبِّرْ ۙ وَ ثِيَابَكَ فَطَهِّرْ ۙ وَ الرُّجْزَ فَاهْجُرْ

"O you who covers himself [with a garment], arise and warn, and glorify your Lord and purify your apparel of the heart, and keep yourself away from the filth [of polytheism]."
(Muddatthir:1-5)

- Given the topics of these surahs, these verses were most likely the Quran's first.

Preaching to his close relatives

- When the Prophet was told to deliver the message, he adopted a gradual process, which was to start from his home and the people near him: only family members and close friends.
- The Prophet only delivered the message according to the instructions and plan given to him by God.
- Some historians have misunderstood this methodology, calling it "secret dawah."

Charity begins at home, but does not end there.

- Since God has guaranteed the protection of His Messengers (Rasool) from enemies, there was no reason for the Prophet to preach in secret. The best way to look at it is that God asked him to start with "Private Dawah" first before reaching out to the public.
- For the first two to three years, he did not preach to the masses. He didn't preach to the pilgrims or visitors to Makkah, or even to some of his own relatives whom he thought would not accept Islam, e.g., Abu Lahab and Abu Jahal.
- They heard about this new theology being preached, but they didn't do anything to the Prophet because he wasn't interfering with trade in Makkah or their other interests.

وَ اَنْذِرْ عَشِيْرَتَكَ الْاَقْرَبِيْنَ ۙ وَ اخْفِضْ جَنَاحَكَ لِمَنِ اتَّبَعَكَ مِنَ الْمُؤْمِنِيْنَ

فَاِنْ عَصَوْكَ فَقُلْ اِنِّيْ بَرِيْٓءٌ مِّمَّا تَعْمَلُوْنَ ۙ وَ تَوَكَّلْ عَلَى الْعَزِيْزِ الرَّحِيْمِ

Warn your closest family members and relatives, and show kindness to the believers who have followed you. And if they disobey you, tell them: 'Indeed, I am disassociated from what you are doing.' And rely upon the Exalted in Might and Merciful. (Surah Shuaraa: 214-217)

Discuss some examples where the "charity begins at home" proverb is applied.

Delivering the Message to Quraysh

- Outside his home, the Prophet had a vast circle of friends, admirers, and well-wishers to whom he began paying attention in order to deliver the message.
- As some of them realized the truth of Islamic teachings, not only did they accept Islam themselves, but they also brought their families and friends into its fold.
- Apart from them, many slaves and underprivileged (poor) people accepted Islam.
- The Prophet first approached the leadership of Quraysh for two main reasons:
    - They were his tribe and people, and he was concerned about them.
    - When you convince the leaders, they will bring their tribesmen into the fold of Islam.
- Initially, the tribe's leaders did not oppose the Prophet's message, but tolerated it because they did not consider it a threat to their beliefs or social fabric.
- The Prophet adopted all possible ways to obey the above instruction in the Quran, including one that was very commonly used among the Arabs. It was a custom amongst them to appoint a guard who would stand on a hill and keep a lookout for any approach from enemies. If he sensed a hostile approach, he would give a loud shout: *Ya Sabaha*! That meant the coming of danger. Hearing this, people would run out from their homes, ask the guard what was amiss, and what the nature of the threat was. If an attack were real, they would prepare accordingly.
- The second time he warned them was when he invited them all to a meal. When they had finished, he tried to address them, but Abu Lahab intervened and said that he was trying to cast his spell over them. He stood up to leave, and others also stood. The Prophet did not get the opportunity to present his invitation.
- The complete conversation for the first incident, where he used the commonly adopted technique to invite everyone, is presented on the next page.

The first warning

- Prophet Muhammad is sent to this world as one who gives glad tidings (good news) and warns. His first warning to his closest people went like this:

The Prophet climbed Mount Safa and said:
"What do you know about me? How do you trust me?"

They said, "We know nothing but good from you — you are our son and the son of our brother; you are our nephew."

He said, "Have you heard any lie from me?"

They said, "We have heard nothing but good. You are al-Amin."

And then the Prophet said, "If I were to tell you that there is an army coming to attack, would you believe me?"

They said, "Yes, we never heard you ever say a lie."

So here is when the Prophet said, "Then know therefore, I am a Warner sent by Allah, to proclaim the coming of severe punishment on the Day of Judgment unless you turn to Allah and leave your idolatry.

Then he called out to various tribes.

"O tribe of Kaab ibn Luay, save yourselves from the Fire of Hell — I will not be able to help you. O Bani Murrah ibn Kaab, save yourselves from the Fire of Hell — I will not be able to help you. [O Bani Kilab ibn Murrah, O Bani Abd Manaf, so on and so forth...]"— until he got to, "O Banu Hashim," and then he began mentioning his uncles and aunts by name, "O Hamzah ibn Abdul Muttalib", "O Safiyyah bint Abdul Muttalib," et al.

And he concluded with the person who was the dearest and most beloved to him, "O Fatima bint Muhammad, you need to save yourself from the Fire of Hell — I will not be able to help you on the Day of Judgment."

The focus of the initial message

- God's message was revealed to the Prophet according to the social and religious conditions of the people (in stages).
- Initially, the oneness of Allah and moral behavior were addressed.
- For example, in the beginning, the following matters were targeted:
  - Believing in one true God with no partners and worshipping Him alone.
  - Awaken the inner goodness of man's nature and create hatred for social evils.
  - Recognition of the rights of others.
  - Taking care of the poor and needy.
  - Kindness to orphans and attention to the principles of morality.
  - Attention to gratitude towards God and earning the pleasures of Jannah.

Respect	Generosity	Caring	Love
Monotheism	Treating others nicely		Sincerity

كَلَّا بَلْ لَّا تُكْرِمُوْنَ الْيَتِيْمَ وَ لَا تَحَٰضُّوْنَ عَلٰى طَعَامِ الْمِسْكِيْنِ وَ تَأْكُلُوْنَ التُّرَاثَ اَكْلًا لَّمًّا

وَّ تُحِبُّوْنَ الْمَالَ حُبًّا جَمًّا

"No! But you do not honor the orphan. And you do not encourage one another to feed the poor. And you consume inheritance, devouring [it] altogether. And you love wealth with immense love." (Surah Fajr:17-20)

اِنَّ سَعْيَكُمْ لَشَتّٰى فَاَمَّا مَنْ اَعْطٰى وَ اتَّقٰى وَ صَدَّقَ بِالْحُسْنٰى فَسَنُيَسِّرُهٗ لِلْيُسْرٰى

وَ اَمَّا مَنْ بَخِلَ وَ اسْتَغْنٰى وَ كَذَّبَ بِالْحُسْنٰى فَسَنُيَسِّرُهٗ لِلْعُسْرٰى

"That your effort is for different ends. Yet he who gives to others, fears God and affirms goodness, We shall ease the way of fortune for him. But he who does not give and is unconcerned, and rejects goodness, is for him. We shall ease the way of adversity." (Surah Layl:4-10)

Find and discuss a few more verses of the Quran, especially in the last Juzz that discusses moral behavior.

Initial reaction from the leaders

- As soon as the Quran began to criticize the guardians of the House of God and their wrong beliefs about worshiping God, and to publicize their wrongdoings, the leaders of the Quraysh openly condemned the teachings and created problems with spreading the message.
- The Quran began to emphasize that they must abandon their previous ways and accept the teachings of Islam, or face the consequences in this life.
- The reason the prophet was asked to start from the leaders was that:
    - They were given the responsibility of keeping the House of God free of any Shirk and clean for Prayers, Eitikaf, Hajj, and animal sacrifice (this was passed down from Prophet Ismail).
    - The people of Arabia regarded them as their religious leaders, and if the Prophet were able to convince them, it would have a broader impact on their followers as well.
- The leaders who refused to heed this message continued to sow confusion and chaos among others through negative propaganda.
- Their main goal was to create distractions rather than challenge the message. They realized that if their followers kept hearing this message and were convinced by it, they would lose their authority and leadership over them.

Methodology adopted

- The methodology adopted by the Prophet is a methodology adopted by all prophets.
- All prophets before Prophet Muhammad were sent to their respective nations and were not tasked with conveying this message to people outside of their nations.
- Although Prophet Muhammad was sent to the entire humanity, he was first asked to share the message with his household before spreading it to others.
- As common Muslims, we have a great lesson in this. If we discover something beneficial for others, we should start by sharing it with those closest to us before sharing it with others (if necessary); otherwise, it's best to keep it within our own circle.
- However, this may not apply to scholars or people learning, as they must also inform the general public.

The All-Wise

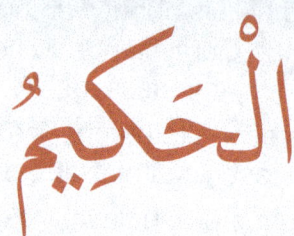

- Allah is All-Wise, meaning none of His actions, no matter how odd/abnormal they appear to us, are devoid of wisdom.

- Sometimes we cannot understand the reasons and motivations behind Allah's actions or decisions because we are short-sighted and unable to see the whole picture.

- Even when Allah says that He is Powerful, He still means that He uses His Power with wisdom.

- Similarly, God advised us that when we must deliver the message of God to someone, we should use wisdom and sincere counsel and argue (only if needed) in the best possible way.

- Being wise in delivering the message means carefully considering the method, timing, situation, and other aspects related to the addressees at the time of delivery.

Call to the way of your Lord with wisdom and good counsel and argue with them in the best possible manner (Surah Nahl: 125).

SEERAH ACTIVITY

POETRY/WRITING COMPETITION

Pick one topic and write a Poem or an Essay on the topic

Topics

1. Allah
2. Creations of Allah
3. Prophet Muhammad before Prophethood
4. Kabaah
5. Prophet Muhammad – A Mercy to Mankind
6. Travel to Taif
7. Hijrah
8. Persecution of Early Muslims

Instructions

- A poem is preferred over an essay.
- Pick a topic that you feel connected to.
- The poem should be between 4 and 8 lines.
- The Essay should be between 6 and 10 lines.
- The central message of the event or topic should be focused on.

Chapter 14

Early Muslims

In this chapter, we will learn about the special people who responded to the call of Islam and accepted the Prophet's Message wholeheartedly.

First people who accepted Islam

- The frontrunners were those who ran towards the true message of Islam as soon as they heard the call of the Prophet Muhammad, without hesitation. The Quran called them *As-Sabiqoon*.
- Although we are calling these people frontrunners, that does not mean that those who accepted the message after thinking it over and hearing the words of the Quran immediately after the frontrunners were less important in the sight of God.

First Muslims

- Khadijah, the prophet's wife (she was the first Muslim)
- Zaynab and Ruqayyah (Prophet's daughters)
- Zaid bin Harithah (his freed slave)
- Ali bin Abi Talib (his very young cousin)
- Abu Bakr As-Siddiq (his close friend)
- Uthman bin Affan
- Zubair bin Al-Awwam
- Abdul Rahman bin Awf
- Saad bin Abi Waqas
- Talha bin Ubaidullah
- Jafar bin Abi Talib and his wife
- Ubaydah bin Harith
- Abu Hudhayfah
- Abu Salamah
- Ayyash bin Rabiyah with his wife
- Arqam bin Abd Munaf
- Asma bint Abi Bakr
- Said bin Zayd with wife Fatimah
- Uthman, Qudamah, and Abdullah bin Mazun
- Abu Ubaydah bin Al-Jarrah
- Abdullah bin Jahash
- Zaynab Bin Jahash
- Khalid bin Said bin Al-Aas

وَّ كُنْتُمْ اَزْوَاجًا ثَلٰثَةً ۚ فَاَصْحٰبُ الْمَيْمَنَةِ ۙ مَاۤ اَصْحٰبُ الْمَيْمَنَةِ ؕ وَ اَصْحٰبُ الْمَشْـَٔمَةِ ۙ مَاۤ اَصْحٰبُ الْمَشْـَٔمَةِ ؕ
وَ السّٰبِقُوْنَ السّٰبِقُوْنَ ۙ اُولٰٓئِكَ الْمُقَرَّبُوْنَ

And you will be in three groups. Then there will be people of the right-hand, and how excellent the people of right-hand are; then there will be people of left-hand, and how unfortunate the people of left-hand are; then there will be frontrunners, who will definitely be frontrunners, they will be the closest to God. (Surah Waqiah: 8-11)

Slaves and Underprivileged

- Many of the converts at the early stage were from the poor class, especially the slaves. Islam appealed to them because of its universal message of protecting human rights and honoring every human being, regardless of social or financial status.

- Before the Quran's revelation, people used to have a very disgraceful attitude towards the poor, orphans, and especially slaves (although people were generally charitable).

- In those times, a human being was judged entirely by their social standing, financial status, physical attributes, tribe/family they belonged to, race, and color.

- The Quran's message brought a shift in this thinking among the new Muslims, and the poor and slaves started seeing the beauty of Islam in this regard.

- They realized that no human being or nation is better than the other; it's our relationship with God and our acts of justice and nobility that make us good or bad in society and in God's sight.

- People began honoring those who were more God-fearing and better informed about Islam – this was a significant change.

- Khabbab bin Al-Arth
- Abdullah bin Masood
- Bilal ibn Rabah
- Ammar bin Yasir
- Sumayyah (wife of Yasir)
- Amir Bin Fahira
- Suhayb Bin Sanan

Interesting question by Heraclius

The first time Prophet Muhammad wrote a letter to Heraclius, the Emperor of Rome, he asked Abu Sufyan 10 questions, and one of those questions was, "Who are his converts? The rich or the weak?" Abu Sufyan said, "The weak and the poor." Heraclius said, "This is the sign of a true faith - it doesn't appeal to the rich or the elite, whereas the poor understand and accept the message."

Value of Early Muslims in the sight of God

- Although we talked about the first Muslims, the early Muslims include all those who accepted Islam within a few years of preaching.
- In fact, the Quran praises all Muslims who accepted Islam while in Makkah before the migration to Medina at many places.
- The reason God praised them was that these people accepted Islam when Muslims and Islam had no position in society. There was nothing positive on the horizon that would attract a person interested only in worldly benefits.
- It also praises those who accepted Islam before the victory of Makkah, because after the victory, Muslims became the dominant force in the region, and many people accepted Islam due to their influence.
- Most of these early Muslims from Makkah later became leaders of the Muslims when the Muslims took over their enemies and achieved a decisive victory over them.
- The people who accepted Islam in the first few years remained faithful to the Prophet through thick and thin.
- Thousands of people accepted Islam after the conquest of Makkah, but most of them were ordinary Muslims, and no one even knows their names now.
- The people called "Sahabi or Sahabiyah" numbered only a few hundred. God gave them this glad tidings that "God is pleased with them, and they are pleased with God" (*Radi-Allah u Anhum Wa Radu Anh*).

وَ مَا لَكُمْ اَلَّا تُنْفِقُوا فِیْ سَبِیْلِ اللّٰهِ وَ لِلّٰهِ مِیْرَاثُ السَّمٰوٰتِ وَ الْاَرْضِ ۖ لَا یَسْتَوِیْ مِنْكُمْ مَّنْ اَنْفَقَ مِنْ قَبْلِ الْفَتْحِ وَ قٰتَلَ ؕ اُولٰٓئِكَ اَعْظَمُ دَرَجَةً مِّنَ الَّذِیْنَ اَنْفَقُوْا مِنْۢ بَعْدُ وَ قٰتَلُوْا ؕ وَ كُلًّا وَّعَدَ اللّٰهُ الْحُسْنٰی ؕ وَ اللّٰهُ بِمَا تَعْمَلُوْنَ خَبِیْرٌ

What has happened to you that you do not spend in the path of Allah, while the heaven and the earth belong to Allah? Remember that among you who spend their wealth in the way of Allah after the victory is not equal in status to those who had spent their wealth in the path of Allah and fought before the victory. Their status will always be higher than the people who spend and fight after the victory. But there is good promise for all of them, and Allah is well aware of your deeds. (Surah Hadeed: 10)

What attracted people to Islam

- The first Muslims looked at the beautiful character of Prophet Muhammad and realized that someone with a lifelong reputation for honesty would not lie about divine revelation.

- The literary beauty and rational appeal of the Quranic verses were another factor that attracted many early Muslims.

- Islam's message of equality strongly appealed to the weak, including slaves, women, and the poor. The Prophet preached against tribal discrimination and for the rights of the weak, offering them a sense of purpose and belonging.

- Islam changed the perspective with which people look at this life and how they should live it.

- Human beings tend to compete with one another in almost everything. While Islam encourages us to participate in healthy competition in our daily lives, it wants us to focus especially on those matters that enhance our chances of earning the best place in the Hereafter.

- Competing over good deeds should be praised and commended. However, even this competition over good deeds should be free of envy or ill feelings toward other Muslims. This was a wholly different, selfless perspective that people of good hearts accepted immediately.

يَٰٓأَيُّهَا ٱلنَّاسُ إِنَّا خَلَقْنَٰكُم مِّن ذَكَرٍ وَّ أُنثَىٰ وَ جَعَلْنَٰكُمْ شُعُوبًا وَّ قَبَآئِلَ لِتَعَارَفُوٓا ۚ إِنَّ أَكْرَمَكُمْ عِندَ ٱللَّهِ أَتْقَىٰكُمْ ۚ إِنَّ ٱللَّهَ عَلِيمٌ خَبِيرٌ

O People, We have created you from one male and one female, and we made you into families and tribes so you can easily recognize each other. The reality is that in the sight of Allah, the most honorable among you is the one who is conscious of God. (Surah Hujraat: 13)

فَٱسْتَبِقُوا ٱلْخَيْرَٰتِ

So, compete with one another in doing good deeds (Surah Baqarah: 148)

The Absolute Truth

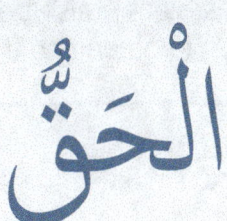

- God called Himself in the Quran, Al-Haqq, the Absolute and Ultimate Truth.
- He is the Truth in His existence, which means that His existence is undeniable (there is enough evidence around us).
- He is also the source of all Truth and Righteousness.
- His Words, the Quran, the Prophets, the Acts, the Reward, the Punishment, Heaven, Hell, Promises, Warnings, etc., are also true.
- When we accept His message, we actually accept the Truth, and that's why anyone at the time of the Prophet who is not arrogant or biased for some reason accepted the message of Islam.

قُلْ مَنْ يَّرْزُقُكُمْ مِّنَ السَّمَآءِ وَ الْأَرْضِ اَمَّنْ يَّمْلِكُ السَّمْعَ وَ الْأَبْصَارَ وَ مَنْ يُّخْرِجُ الْحَيَّ مِنَ الْمَيِّتِ وَ يُخْرِجُ الْمَيِّتَ مِنَ الْحَيِّ وَ مَنْ يُّدَبِّرُ الْأَمْرَ ۚ فَسَيَقُولُونَ اللهُ ۚ فَقُلْ اَفَلَا تَتَّقُونَ فَذٰلِكُمُ اللهُ رَبُّكُمُ الْحَقُّ ۚ فَمَا ذَا بَعْدَ الْحَقِّ اِلَّا الضَّلٰلُ ۚ فَاَنّٰى تُصْرَفُونَ

Ask them who gives you your provisions from the sky and the earth. Who controls your hearing and sight? Who gives life to the dead and brings death to life? Who is controlling the affairs of this world? They will surely say, It's Allah, then why don't you fear Him? So, know that this is your Lord, the Truth. So, other than misguidance, what do you have after seeing this Truth? Then, where are you turning? (Surah Younus: 32)

Why does Islam praise people who are always ahead in good deeds? Why is it so difficult to be among the first?

SEERAH ACTIVITY

SAHABI CARDS

Create "Sahabi Cards" that highlight two to three key attributes or qualities for which they are known. Build as many as you can and put them on a poster.

Example

Abu Bakr (RA)

1) First Caliph of Muslims
2) A very kind and soft-hearted friend of Prophet Muhammad
3) He was with the Prophet during Hijrah.

Chapter 15

Persecution in the path of Truth

In this chapter, we will learn about the persecution of Muslims at the hands of the leaders of Quraish in the beginning, when Prophet Muhammad started preaching the message.

A grave test for the first believers begin

- After an initial dull reaction, the leaders of the Quraysh soon realized:
    - It was hitting hard on the polytheistic way of life – financial and cultural impact.
    - The message of Islam is very appealing, and people are now paying attention to it.
    - The Quran's language is unique, and it contains great wisdom.
    - The tribal system was the main obstacle to the idea of punishing every convert.
- Since most of the early converts were weak, poor, and young people, the quickest way to prevent a large upset in society was to inflict hardships on weak and young people and make life difficult for them.
- Tribal elders were tasked with disciplining their own members.
- The Quran asked the early Muslims to remain steadfast and patient; if they did so, they would be rewarded immensely in the Hereafter, and it gave them examples from the past.
- When young people confronted their parents, the Quran told them that they must deal with their parents kindly, without agreeing with them on this matter.

The Sacrifices

- This was the worst period when the faith of almost all the new Muslims was tested one way or the other; Yasir and his wife, Sumayyah, also lost their lives.

- Umayyah Bin Khalaf used to torture Bilal Ibn Rabah in the blazing sun while he was lying on the hot sand of Arabia with no food or water.
- Sumayyah bint Khayyat got tortured along with her husband Yasir, and they both sacrificed their lives but did not forsake their religion.
- Abu Bakr and other affluent Muslims like him bought many slaves and gave them freedom from this misery.

We live in a free world, but Muslims still face problems due to their faith. Discuss some of the challenges that Muslims face today.

Techniques used by the disbelievers

1 The tribal elders and leaders were tasked with disciplining people within their tribes, and slaves were their property. That was the first approach taken. Some of the stories mentioned in the history book are horrifying and shocking.

2 They were not only tortured/abused physically but emotionally as well.

3 Converts who were traders were barred from selling their produce in the market; laborers, after finishing their jobs, were deprived of their wages.

4 They started spreading the message that Muhammad was humiliating their gods and religion and calling them man-made. It was a disgrace to hear such an insult towards the religion of their forefathers. They wanted to incite their people by exploiting their sense of belonging and attachment to their culture.

5 Those who had some status in society were physically attacked and harmed in the dark of the night.

6 Extended families boycotted the converts and refused to give their daughters from their families to marry; it was a social boycott.

God told Muslims in the Quran that people before them had to endure much more difficult situations than those they faced. It is God's practice to judge the faith of the Prophet's companions through such trials. The purpose is to identify hypocrites and to know who is ready to support the Prophet and who is not.

أَمْ حَسِبْتُمْ أَنْ تَدْخُلُوا الْجَنَّةَ وَ لَمَّا يَأْتِكُمْ مَّثَلُ الَّذِينَ خَلَوْا مِنْ قَبْلِكُمْ ۖ مَسَّتْهُمُ الْبَأْسَاءُ وَ الضَّرَّاءُ وَ زُلْزِلُوا حَتَّى يَقُولَ الرَّسُولُ وَ الَّذِينَ أَمَنُوا مَعَهُ مَتَى نَصْرُ اللهِ ۗ أَلَا إِنَّ نَصْرَ اللهِ قَرِيبٌ

Or do you think you will enter Paradise while such [trial] has not yet come to you as came to those who came before you? They were touched by poverty and hardship and were shaken until [even their] messenger and those who believed with him said, "When is the help of Allah going to come?" No doubt, the help of Allah is near. (Surah Baqarah: 214)

وَ لَيَعْلَمَنَّ اللهُ الَّذِينَ أَمَنُوا وَ لَيَعْلَمَنَّ الْمُنْفِقِينَ

And God will clearly differentiate between those who believe and those who are hypocrites. (Surah Ankabot: 11)

Influencing Prophet Muhammad

Quraysh approached Abu Talib

- A select elite group of leaders went to Abu Talib and complained about Prophet Muhammad's activities and the threat that he was posing to the religion of their forefathers.
- They threatened both Abu Talib and Muhammad with dire consequences.
- Abu Talib presented this issue before Prophet Muhammad and asked his nephew not to burden him with the responsibility of protecting him.
- Prophet Muhammad recognized his uncle's situation, yet he expressed his resolve, saying he would not abandon this responsibility even if it cost him his life.
- Seeing his nephew's determination, Abu Talib told him to go ahead with his activities, promising to stand by him, come what may.
- The Quraish also offered to Abu Talib / Banu Hashim to hand over Prophet Muhammad in exchange for a person from among their own, suggesting that they themselves could kill Muhammad while Abu Talib / Banu Hasim could kill one of theirs.

A Conversation with Utbah

- Utbah bin Rabiah, an important, influential, well-read, and wealthy leader of Quraysh, approached Prophet Muhammad with an offer.
- Utbah complained about the 'disunity' that Prophet Muhammad had caused among his people and offered him the following if he stopped:
  - If you need wealth, we will collect it from the tribes and give you as much as you need.
  - If you need status, we will designate you as our leader and obey you.
  - If you want the throne, we will make you our king.
  - If you are under the spell of someone, we will help you get treated for that.
- Instead of responding to him, the Prophet recited Surah Fussilat to him (verses 1-13). When the prophet reached verse 13, Utbah screamed, demanding that the prophet stop.
- He told Quraysh his impression of the Quran. It is neither poetry nor magic, nor even old stories. Leave Muhammad alone because 'this thing' is going to overpower everything. They blamed Utbah for being under the spell of Muhammad.

If they turn away, tell them I warn you with a lightning strike like the one that struck Aad and Thamud. (Surah Fussilat: 13)

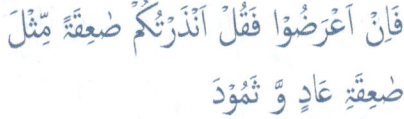

فَاِنْ اَعْرَضُوْا فَقُلْ اَنْذَرْتُكُمْ صٰعِقَةً مِّثْلَ صٰعِقَةِ عَادٍ وَّ ثَمُوْدَ

Dar-al-Arqam and its Significance

- When Musa and the Children of Israel were persecuted at the hands of the Pharaoh, God instructed them to make the houses of Musa and Haroon as their central place of meeting (also Qiblah for prayers).

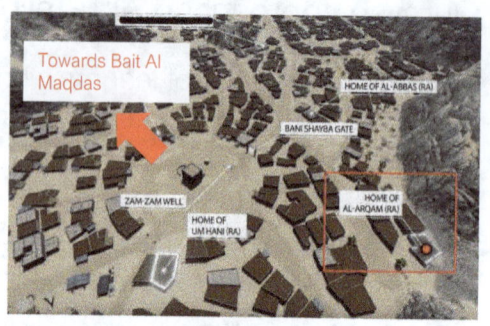

- The new Muslims found themselves in a similar situation, and Prophet Muhammad designated the home of Arqam bin Abd Munaf for the same purpose.

- All new converts would gather there, perform collective prayers, learn the Quran, and seek strength and guidance from the Prophet's teachings.

- The house of Al-Arqam became the first center of learning for the new faith's followers.

- The house of Al-Arqam was situated south of Kabaah, and Prophet Muhammad could face both Kabaah and Bayt al-Maqdas at the same time when praying in the house.

- Due to the fear of persecution, some new converts, especially those young and weak, were allowed to hide their Islam. But that was not the case with Prophet Muhammad. However, the new Muslims behave differently in this situation.

Strong Believers

- People were searching for the truth even before Prophet Muhammad announced his prophethood. They found nothing strange in his message and accepted it with a full heart, holding it dear. All early converts fall into this group.

Reflective Believers

- Those who sought logic and reason in any message they heard reflected on the arguments the Prophet presented.

- They carefully considered their past and present lives and affairs, and the consequences of accepting the message, before making the decision.

Weak Believers

- They accepted the message under external pressure but were unaware of the demands it could place on them. Soon, they began feeling pressure from their elders and tribesmen, faced active opposition, and grew nervous.

First Migration to Abyssinia

- God showed the believers a way out. In case they decide to leave the city and go somewhere else where they can worship God freely, God will help them.

- When the oppression by the Quraysh became unbearable for certain people, Prophet Muhammad allowed them to migrate to Abyssinia. The Christian ruler of Abyssinia was famous for his kindness and fairness.

- The Prophet had already known that the king of Abyssinia, *Najashi* (Ashamah Negus), was a fair ruler who would not wrong any of the Muslims.

- Eleven men and five women made up the first group who migrated.

- Most people were afraid of migration due to immediate financial hardships and the challenges of a new environment.

- They sneaked out of Makkah in the middle of the night and headed for the sea, where two boats happened to be sailing for Abyssinia (Ethiopia), their destination.

- When word got out in Abyssinia that the first group had been received well, many people began moving out of Makkah and made the migration (a total of around 80 people).

- Some famous names who did the first migration were: Uthman bin Affan with his wife, Zubair bin Al-Awwam, Musab bin Umair, Abu Salamah with his wife Umm Salamah, Jafar bin Abi Talib with his wife Asma, Khalid bin Said bin Al-Aas, Abu Ubaydah bin Al-Jarrah, Abdullah bin Masood, and Abu Musa Al-Ashari.

يٰعِبَادِىَ الَّذِيْنَ اٰمَنُوْٓا اِنَّ اَرْضِيْ وَاسِعَةٌ فَاِيَّاىَ فَاعْبُدُوْنِ ۚ كُلُّ نَفْسٍ ذَآئِقَةُ الْمَوْتِ ۚ ثُمَّ اِلَيْنَا تُرْجَعُوْنَ
وَ الَّذِيْنَ اٰمَنُوْا وَ عَمِلُوا الصّٰلِحٰتِ لَنُبَوِّئَنَّهُمْ مِّنَ الْجَنَّةِ غُرَفًا تَجْرِىْ مِنْ تَحْتِهَا الْاَنْهٰرُ خٰلِدِيْنَ فِيْهَا ۚ نِعْمَ اَجْرُ الْعٰمِلِيْنَ
الَّذِيْنَ صَبَرُوْا وَ عَلٰى رَبِّهِمْ يَتَوَكَّلُوْنَ وَ كَاَيِّنْ مِّنْ دَآبَّةٍ لَّا تَحْمِلُ رِزْقَهَا ۖ اَللّٰهُ يَرْزُقُهَا وَ اِيَّاكُمْ ۖ وَ هُوَ السَّمِيْعُ الْعَلِيْمُ

My servants who have believed, [if these people do not desist from oppressing you, migrate from this place], indeed, vast is My land; so, worship Me only. Every soul must taste death. Then you will be returned to Us alone, and those who have accepted faith and have done righteous deeds, We shall definitely give them a place in the tall mansions of Paradise, below which streams shall be flowing; they shall abide in them forever. What a nice reward for those who labor, who were steadfast and used to trust their Lord in all circumstances. How many animals roam about without carrying their sustenance. Only God gives them sustenance, and to you too, and He hears and knows all.

Quraysh's Response

- News of their departure at night reached the ears of Quraish, so some men were sent out in their pursuit, but the believers had already left by the time they reached the port.
- Quraysh decided to follow the Muslims to persuade the king to return them.
- They sent Amr Bin Al-Aas and Abdullah bin Abi Rabiah with gifts to present their case in front of the king:

"O King, a few silly young men have come to your country. They have left the faith of their ancestors and have not accepted your faith. They present a new religion that neither you nor we are familiar with. Their elders have sent us to you to request you to send them back to them because only they can keep an eye on them."

- After consulting with his courtiers, the king decided to listen to these migrant Muslims before making a decision. **Jafar Bin Abi Talib** presented his case, which convinced the King not to hand them over.

- "O' King, before we accepted this new faith, we were idol worshippers, consumed by dead meat, cut off connections with our blood relations, and engaged in indecent and immoral activities.
- God sent His messenger among us. We were already well aware of his dignified lineage, truthfulness, piety, and honesty.
- He called us to worship one God and stop praying to man-made idols.
- He taught us to speak the truth, deal honestly with others, have mercy on our fellow human beings, be kind to our neighbors, perform our prayers, pay charity, and avoid polytheism.
- He instructed us to abstain from lying, cheating, taking away the rights of orphans, indecent acts, and all other actions that could obstruct us from living a pious life.
- We witnessed what he said was the truth, confirmed our faith in his message, and followed his instructions.
- Our countrymen have brought great trials upon us; they have tortured us, penalized us, and tried their utmost to turn us away from our faith. When living in our own country became impossible, we came to yours, choosing it as a safe haven. We hope that we shall not find any injustice here."

A tactic played by the delegation

- The delegation of Quraysh then decided to incite the king based on his religious feelings about Jesus (because the king was a Christian).
- They told the king that Muhammad and his followers were disrespectful to Christianity and that they were presenting the wrong idea about Jesus, which was entirely against his beliefs.
- The king asked the Muslims what they think of Jesus in their religion?
- Jafar responded by reciting the story of Jesus and Mary from Surah Maryam, stating that Muslims believe in Jesus and that Jesus was God's servant and a prophet.
- The king and his courtiers were so impressed by the verses of the Quran that he acknowledged that Jesus was no more than what Muslims thought of him and that their belief was true.
- The delegation from Quraysh returned without achieving its objectives. The king told the Muslims that they could stay in his country as long as they wished.
- In this way, Quraish's bad intentions to evict Muslims from the land met with utter failure. They came to fully realize that the hatred they nursed against the Muslims would not work beyond Makkah.

Situation of Christianity at that time

- At that time, many Christians were not satisfied with the beliefs of the Trinity and Jesus being the Son of God. They were waiting for the last prophet, as Jesus himself predicted.
- When they heard about the last prophet, they wanted to inquire more. A group of 20 Christians from Abyssinia visited Makkah to conduct their investigations and ask questions.
- When they were convinced about the last prophet, they immediately accepted Islam and returned to share this with their king and others.
- Later, Prophet Muhammad wrote a letter to the king, who accepted Islam. The Quraysh became angry at this and began keeping an eye on visitors entering Makkah.

In our times when there is no Prophet among us, is it OK to hide our faith if we are afraid for our lives because of that?

Few Notable Conversions

- Early in the preaching phase in Makkah, two prominent figures accepted Islam, which slightly altered the power dynamics in Makkah. In this section, we will discuss a few conversions.

Hamzah Bin Abdul Muttalib

- Once, close to Mount Safa, Abu Jahal picked up an argument with the Prophet in which he verbally abused the Prophet and cursed at him while the Prophet remained silent.
- Some freed slave girls witnessed this incident and told Hamzah about it when he returned from a hunting trip.
- Hamzah got upset that Abu Jahal mistreated his nephew. He reached him and hit him with his bow's head and said, "You have abused my nephew while I am also of his faith. If you are brave enough, come and fight with me."
- Hamzah later admitted that although he had not accepted his nephew's faith, he had said so in the heat of the moment. Later, Hamzah himself converted to Islam and proved to be a great follower of Islam who gave his life in the Battle of Uhud for the sake of his faith.

Abu Dharr Ghafari

- Abu Dharr, from the Ghifar tribe, learned that someone in Makkah had claimed prophethood. Abu Dharr decided to travel to Makkah himself.
- Ali Bin Abi Talib hosted him for three days. When he told Ali about the purpose of his visit, Ali took him directly to Prophet Muhammad.
- He immediately accepted Islam and decided to announce it publicly in front of the Kabaah. People from Quraysh attacked him and beat him up.
- The Prophet's uncle warned Quraysh that the tribe of Ghifar was situated on the trade route to Syria, and if something happened to Abu Dharr, his tribe would make the trade trips difficult for them.
- This incident shows that Quraysh had created an environment of fear and hostility towards visitors, especially if they came to meet the Prophet.

Omar bin Al-Khattab accepts Islam

- The Prophet was praying to God to strengthen Islam through one of the Omars (bin Al-Khattab or bin Al-Hisham). Omar bin Al-Hisham was Abu Jahal.

- There are a couple of narrations about Omar Al-Khattab's conversion.

- **First Narration:** It is said that due to the growing disunity among the tribes after the spread of Islam, Omar bin Al-Khattab decided to kill the Prophet. On his way to the Prophet, someone told him that his own sister had already converted. He rushed to his sister's house, and after an interaction with his Muslim sister, his heart turned towards Islam upon hearing the verses of Surah Taha she was reciting.

- **Second Narration:** Once Omar bin Al-Khattab visited Umm Abdullah and her family, they decided to migrate to Abyssinia. Umm Abdullah told Omar they were leaving because of the pain and suffering that people like Omar himself had caused them. She told him they wanted to leave the city to worship God freely. Omar felt ashamed and left, saying, "May God be with you."

- Then, one night, Omar went to the Kabaah for Tawaf and found the Prophet reciting Surah Haaqqah. He hid behind the cloth of the Kabaah and listened to this recitation. He thought these were the words of a poet, and Prophet Muhammad recited verse 41 of Surah Haaqqah. Then he thought these must be the words of magic, and Prophet Muhammad recited verse 42. He experienced as if God was listening to his thoughts and responding to him through the Quran.

- He was amazed, and when the Prophet headed towards his home, Omar followed and accepted Islam there.

- Omar's coming into Islam changed the situation of Muslims in Makkah. They used to pray in hiding, but after Omar accepted Islam, they started praying in the Kabaah.

"O Allah, strengthen Islam with Abu Jahl bin Hisham or Umar bin Al-Khattab." In the morning, Umar bin Al-Khattab went to the Prophet and embraced Islam. [Sunan Tirmidhi, Hadith 3683]

It is reported that Jibrael descended and said to the Prophet: "O Muhammad – may Allah send greetings and salutations on him – indeed, the residents of the heavens are rejoicing in Umar`s embracing Islam." [Sunan Ibn Majah, Hadith 103]

Revelation about Romans

- Right around that time, an interesting incident happened that was recorded in the Quran, and God also made a prediction about it.
- In Surah Rum, God said:

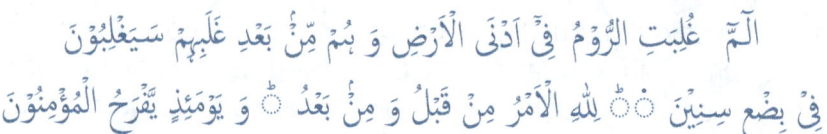

الٓمّٓ ۚ غُلِبَتِ الرُّوْمُ ۙ فِیْۤ اَدْنَی الْاَرْضِ وَ هُمْ مِّنْ بَعْدِ غَلَبِهِمْ سَیَغْلِبُوْنَ

فِیْ بِضْعِ سِنِیْنَ ۚ۬ لِلّٰهِ الْاَمْرُ مِنْ قَبْلُ وَ مِنْ بَعْدُ ۚ وَ یَوْمَئِذٍ یَّفْرَحُ الْمُؤْمِنُوْنَ

This is Surah Alif Lam Meem. The Byzantines have been defeated in the nearest land. But after their defeat, they will overcome within three to nine years. To God belongs the command before and after, and that day, the believers will rejoice in the victory of God (Surah Rum: 1-4)

- On the one hand, the episode of Abyssinia created hatred and bitterness among the Quraysh for Christians.
- On the other hand, Muslims were deeply grateful to the Christians and naturally felt inclined toward them.
- Outside the Arab world, in 616 AD, the great empires of Persia (Polytheists) and Rome (Christians) fought a war in which Persia invaded a part of Roman land and seemed to have an upper hand.
- The Persian King, Khusru Pervaiz, started dreaming about overpowering the Romans after this small gain.
- When the news reached Makkah, Quraysh was jubilant over this and started taunting the Muslims and threatening them with the same fate in the end.
- God, in Surah Rum, revealed this incident and predicted that, within 9-11 years, the situation would be reversed, and the Romans would regain dominance over their enemies.
- The prediction came true: Right around that time when Muslims defeated the Quraish in the Battle of Badr, the Romans defeated the Persians and regained control of the land. This gave Muslims a sense of relief and a message of their eventual victory over Quraysh.
- This not only strengthened the belief of the Muslims but also caused other people to think about Islam.

Return of the Migrants

- After staying in Abyssinia for a few years, around 33-40 Muslims, including some wives, returned to Makkah due to some misinformation spread among them.

- It is reported that due to the acceptance of Islam by Omar and Hamza, they heard that the situation for the Muslims had improved and decided to come back.

- After leaving their homes, they realized the situation was not as good as they had initially thought and sought protection from other tribes before entering the city.

- In tribal societies, when someone takes someone under their protection, the safety of that person becomes their responsibility, even if they have to fight to uphold it.

- People like Walid Bin Mughirah, Abu Lahab, and Abu Jahal were unhappy with this arrangement and persuaded the tribal elders to withdraw their protection.

- The Muslims who had migrated to Abyssinia later migrated again to Medina and received God's blessings for a double migration in the way of God.

- In Islam, migrating to another land to practice one's religion in the sight of God is considered one of the righteous deeds.

- In conclusion, we must realize that we are all tested by God in this life. However, the tests of the Prophets and the people around them are unique and much more severe.

- Many people ask if God loves His prophets and believers, why they go through such difficult situations, and why victory does not come immediately.

- The reward for Prophets and his companions, for remaining steadfast throughout their struggles, is immense. It is not the kind of reward that is granted to everyone.

- God responded to this question in the Quran in Surah Al-Ankabut:

أَحَسِبَ النَّاسُ أَنْ يُتْرَكُوا أَنْ يَقُولُوا آمَنَّا وَ هُمْ لَا يُفْتَنُونَ

وَ لَقَدْ فَتَنَّا الَّذِينَ مِنْ قَبْلِهِمْ فَلَيَعْلَمَنَّ اللهُ الَّذِينَ صَدَقُوا وَ لَيَعْلَمَنَّ الْكَذِبِينَ

Do the people think they will be left after saying, "We believe," and they will not be tried? Certainly, We have tried people before them, and We will surely make it clear who are truthful in their belief, and He will surely make it clear who are the liars. (Surah Al-Ankabut: 2-3)

The Most Powerful

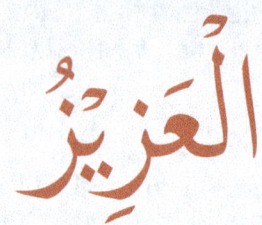

- Al-Azeez is the one whose power is overwhelming with the strength and glory that He deserves, and no one can stop Him.

- God is Mighty, Powerful, and Strong, and Exalted due to this Might.

- In the Quran, His name Al-Azeez is often paired with Al-Hakeem (The All-Wise), which means He uses His Power wisely when and where it is needed.

- In the Quran, God also said that all Might and all Honor belong to Him.

- He sometimes lets us go through difficult situations, which He can change immediately through His Power, but He does not, because most of the time, the best form within us comes out in difficult situations.

- Sometimes, His help is delayed. We cannot comprehend because we are short-sighted and cannot see the entire picture. He is in control of the situation and has the bigger picture in mind.

فَلِلّٰهِ الْحَمْدُ رَبِّ السَّمٰوٰتِ وَ رَبِّ الْأَرْضِ رَبِّ الْعٰلَمِيْنَ

وَ لَهُ الْكِبْرِيَآءُ فِى السَّمٰوٰتِ وَ الْأَرْضِ ۚ وَ هُوَ الْعَزِيْزُ الْحَكِيْمُ

Hence, gratitude is for God alone, Lord of the heavens and Lord of the earth; Lord of the entire universe. His is the sovereignty in the heavens and the earth, and He is Powerful, very Wise. (45:36-37)

SEERAH ACTIVITY

HANDWRITE A LETTER

"Handwrite a Letter" to the persecuted Muslims in Makkah and tell them what they should do and how you feel about them, sympathize with them, and empathize with them. Relate it to people in today's world and how they face persecution even today.

Instructions

- The letter should <u>not</u> be typed on a computer.
- The letter should be between 300 and 500 words (not more than a standard-sized page).

Chapter 16

Objections and Opposition

In this chapter, we will learn about the types of objections raised by the disbelievers, the kind of opposition they imposed on Muslims, and how the Quran responded to every objection.

Objections raised and the Quran's responses

Various Seerah writers document numerous objections raised by the Quraish against Prophet Muhammad and the Quran during the Meccan period. These objections ranged from personal slanders to disputes over belief, the Quranic style, and socio-economic fears.

Objection 1 – The Quran is poetry and storytelling

- In the beginning, the verses of the Quran were short and rhyming, yet delivered a powerful message in precise, complete sentences (for example, the verses below).
- Short verses can also give an impression of prose (text) read in rhythm.
- The style of the Quran is somewhere between poetry and prose (text), which is a unique style.
- Arab writers were familiar with different literary styles and were great critics of them.
- The Quran's style demonstrated the beauty and miraculous nature of this book to its direct audience.
- Since they could distinguish between good and bad poetry, they were pretty astonished by the beauty of the Quran and were confused about which category to put this piece of literature in.
- Magicians and fortune-tellers also used such short, rhythmic sentences in those times, so the Quraysh initially claimed that the Prophet was learning them from magicians and soothsayers.
- They backed their argument by saying that a "Jinn" comes and teaches the Prophet poetry and news about the future (because they heard that an angel comes to teach him these verses).

كَلَّا وَالْقَمَرِ . وَالَّيْلِ اِذْ اَدْبَرَ . وَالصُّبْحِ اِذَآ اَسْفَرَ . اِنَّهَا لَاِحْدَى الْكُبَرِ . نَذِيْرًا لِّلْبَشَرِ . لِمَنْ شَآءَ مِنْكُمْ اَنْ يَّتَقَدَّمَ اَوْ يَتَاَخَّرَ . (٧٤:٣٢-٣٧)

اِذَا السَّمَآءُ انْفَطَرَتْ . وَاِذَا الْكَوَاكِبُ انْتَثَرَتْ . وَاِذَا الْبِحَارُ فُجِّرَتْ . وَاِذَا الْقُبُوْرُ بُعْثِرَتْ . عَلِمَتْ نَفْسٌ مَّا قَدَّمَتْ وَاَخَّرَتْ . (٨٢:١-٥)

> The Quran is not poetry, but its verses rhyme. What is the benefit of this kind of rhyming?

Quran's Response – Why the Quran is not poetry and storytelling

- The predictions of the fortune-tellers are vague and usually carry double meanings, and most of the words of the magicians are meaningless.
- Poets are often unconcerned with the facts of life. They usually take you to a world you dream of living in. They do not do what they say because their poetry is for others.
- Since Arabs were aware of such literature, it was one of the most straightforward objections that Quraysh raised against the Quran to target it for propaganda.
- It was a shot in the dark by the Quraysh because they were desperate to dishonor and belittle the Quran.
- The focus of the initial verses was on the unseen but real world that is about to come, which is a serious matter:
  - The end of this worldly life
  - The events that will occur after death
  - The accountability of human beings for their actions
  - Final reward and punishment
- Every word in the Quran is thoughtful, has deep meaning, points to the realities of human life and existence, and appeals to the heart.
- The Quran had a target audience, and many accepted the message just because of its miraculous language and style.
- Its message is consistent, but delivered in different ways and styles.
- It does not compromise on fundamentals such as the unity of God and the Hereafter.
- The Prophet practiced what he said, and he followed a strict moral code of beliefs and actions.
- The Quran encourages charity, moral integrity, caring for relatives and other human beings, virtues like sacrifice and selflessness, goodness and piety, etc.
- Many pious and honest people, already known for a trait admired by human beings, accepted Islam at the very beginning.
- Only arrogant, immoral people did not admire the message of the Quran and became its enemies.

> One might ask, why would evil forces bring such a positive message to humanity?

Objection 2 – Quran is a human effort

- Quraysh realized very early that the Quran's content was unique and that no human being could produce it without 'external' help (probably from a Christian).
- The tribal leaders tried to convince people that it was Muhammad who was fabricating this message with someone's help, and there was no reason to believe that there was any divine source behind it.
- When their story of the Jinns and soothsayers did not sell, they claimed that non-Arabs, and especially the People of the Book, were helping him because they were aware of such books.
- They claimed that these people create a piece of the Quran and then present it in the name of God when it's ready.

Quran's Response – Why the Quran is not a human effort

- The Quran was revealed in the purest form of Arabic and in the language of Quraysh, making it impossible for it to have been created by non-Arabs or the People of the Book.
- Quraysh had the best poets among them, and it was not difficult for them to produce something like the Quran to disprove the Quran's divinity, but they could not.
- The Quran was revealed gradually. It was revealed, according to the situation and circumstances, that answering the questions raised by its addressees – it is only God who is aware of all these situations and questions raised.
- The guidance provided by the Quran in different circumstances came only as needed, making it a living book among them.
- The message of the Quran is still relevant today, which would not have been possible if a human had written it.
- The Prophet did not write anything before the age of 40.

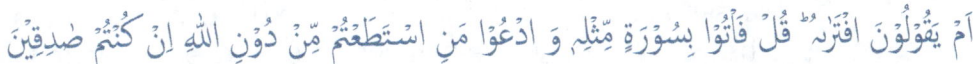

اَمْ يَقُولُونَ افْتَرَاهُ قُلْ فَأْتُوا بِسُورَةٍ مِّثْلِهِ وَ ادْعُوا مَنِ اسْتَطَعْتُمْ مِّنْ دُونِ اللهِ اِنْ كُنْتُمْ صٰدِقِينَ

Do they say: "The Prophet has fabricated it?" Tell them: If you are truthful, bring forth a surah like it and call [to help] whoever you can except God. (Surah Yunus: 38)

Objection 3 – Quran is magic

- The Quran attracted people's hearts and minds through its beauty, expression, and the simplicity of its message, which goes well with human nature.
- In a way, people listening to the Quran were spellbound and would sacrifice everything for the faith.
- Due to these characteristics, Quraysh began spreading the rumor that the Prophet was practicing magic through the Quran.
- Simple people were affected by this propaganda, but thoughtful people were not.

Quran's Response – Why the Quran is not magic

- Magic's influence is temporary.
- Magic is usually based on lies, and it makes things appear the way the magicians want them to appear.
- The change that the Quran brought into people's lives was permanent, and they were ready to die for it. The Quran created lofty characters like Omar, Abu Bakr, Uthman, Ali, Bilal, etc., which no magic can create.
- The Quran is the truth to its core and has come to destroy every falsehood.
- The true nature and status of the Quran's message and its content have been clarified in several places, which explains why it is not magic.
- Several verses describe what the Quran is, who brings it, what its source is, and how it is delivered to the heart of the Prophet.
- The Quran appealed to the people to give up their racial and tribal biases and open their minds and hearts to ponder over its message.

فَلَآ أُقْسِمُ بِمَا تُبْصِرُوْنَ وَ مَا لَا تُبْصِرُوْنَ إِنَّهُ لَقَوْلُ رَسُوْلٍ كَرِيْمٍ وَّ مَا هُوَ بِقَوْلِ شَاعِرٍ ۚ قَلِيْلًا مَّا تُؤْمِنُوْنَ

وَ لَا بِقَوْلِ كَاهِنٍ ۚ قَلِيْلًا مَّا تَذَكَّرُوْنَ تَنْزِيْلٌ مِّنْ رَّبِّ الْعٰلَمِيْنَ

"So, I swear by what you see. And what you do not see [that] indeed, the Quran is the word of a noble Messenger. And it is not the word of a poet; little do you believe. Nor the word of a soothsayer; little do you remember. [It is] a revelation from the Lord of the Worlds." (Surah Haqqah:38-43)

Objection 4 – Prophet is just a human being

- Seeing the Prophet as an ordinary man with a brilliant character, the Quraysh attempted to cast a shadow over the fact that Muhammad was God's Prophet.
- They saw his life as no different from any other human being, and they used this argument as propaganda against him – why was he just a usual human being like them, going through the challenges of life?
- Later, they added the allegation that, since he could not become a successful trader or a leader in society, he was doing so to become one of the elite of Quraysh.
- The Banu Umayyah tribe had rivaled the Banu Hashim in every aspect of life, but now they could not tolerate the Banu Hashim having prophethood, and they did not – it made them the Banu Hashim's fierce opponents.
- They also questioned why Muhammad was selected for prophethood while 'better' and more influential people existed among them.
- They also argued that it was not befitting for a human to become a messenger; an angel should do this job.

Quran's Response – ALL Prophets were human beings

- Quraysh knew very well that all prophets were human beings. The People of the Book have also been told that Ibrahim, Ismail, Ishaq, Yaqoob, Musa, and Jesus were all human beings.
- Their family lineage went back to Prophet Ibrahim, and they were proud to be linked to such a noble ancestor. They were following the religion of Ibrahim without realizing that certain innovations had been introduced by their forefathers who came after Ismail.
- A different creation could not be sent to human beings for guidance, because it would never serve as an example to humans. Only a human being could relate to the problems and challenges of another human being. That is why prophets could only explain issues related to human beings.
- God explained in the Quran: Had angels been living on this earth and God had desired to guide them, He would have sent an angel to guide them.

Why is it important that a prophet must be a human being?

وَ مَا مَنَعَ النَّاسَ اَنْ يُؤْمِنُوٓا اِذْ جَآءَهُمُ الْهُدٰى اِلَّاۤ اَنْ قَالُوٓا اَبَعَثَ اللّٰهُ بَشَرًا رَّسُوْلًا

قُلْ لَّوْ كَانَ فِي الْاَرْضِ مَلٰٓئِكَةٌ يَّمْشُوْنَ مُطْمَئِنِّيْنَ لَنَزَّلْنَا عَلَيْهِمْ مِّنَ السَّمَآءِ مَلَكًا رَّسُوْلًا

"And what prevented the people from believing when the guidance came to them except that they said: 'Has God sent a human messenger?' Say: "If there were upon the earth angels walking securely, We would have sent down to them from the Heaven, an angel [as a] messenger." (Surah Bani Israel:94-95)

اَكَانَ لِلنَّاسِ عَجَبًا اَنْ اَوْحَيْنَاۤ اِلٰى رَجُلٍ مِّنْهُمْ اَنْ اَنْذِرِ النَّاسَ وَ بَشِّرِ الَّذِيْنَ اٰمَنُوٓا اَنَّ لَهُمْ قَدَمَ صِدْقٍ عِنْدَ رَبِّهِمْ ۗ قَالَ الْكٰفِرُوْنَ اِنَّ هٰذَا لَسٰحِرٌ مُّبِيْنٌ

Were these people overcome with wonder that We have sent Our revelation to a human person from among them: "Warn people and give glad tidings to those who believe that for them is a position of great honor with their Lord." [Instead of understanding this fact,] these disbelievers said: "This person is an expert magician."(Surah Yunus:2)

قُلْ اِنَّمَاۤ اَنَا بَشَرٌ مِّثْلُكُمْ يُوْحٰىۤ اِلَيَّ اَنَّمَاۤ اِلٰهُكُمْ اِلٰهٌ وَّاحِدٌ ۚ فَمَنْ كَانَ يَرْجُوْا لِقَآءَ رَبِّهٖ فَلْيَعْمَلْ عَمَلًا صَالِحًا وَّ لَا يُشْرِكْ بِعِبَادَةِ رَبِّهٖۤ اَحَدًا

Say (O Muhammad), I am nothing but a human being like you, except that the revelation is sent to me that your Lord is one Lord. So, whoever is hoping to meet his Lord should work righteous deeds and should never worship anyone besides Him (Surah Kahf:110)

Objection 5 – The lack of Worldly Goods

- The Prophet led a very humble life. The non-believers argued that if God had to bless someone with prophethood, He could have given him worldly goods and riches to elevate his status and influence in society, or God should have chosen a more influential person for this job.

- They said that some hasty youth and poor slaves had gathered around him, but no 'wise' leader had joined him, and one of the reasons for that was the lack of any financial standing.

- They insisted that they would only listen to him when his poor companions were not with him.

- They used to get upset at verses that foretold that these poor companions would be the future leaders and that the leaders of the Quraysh would be thrown in Hellfire if they continued to reject.
- At one point, Quraysh made miraculous demands of the Prophet:
  - Create a freshwater spring in the water-scarce land or obtain for himself an oasis and a garden with waterways running through its center.
  - A garden providing him with riches (including harvests) of all types.
  - Ask God to make a palace of gold for him.
  - Make some pieces of the sky fall on them.
  - Angels should come down and be visible to them, or why could he not climb up to the Heavens in front of them?
  - Go up to the Heavens and bring a written revelation to them.

Quran's Response – Religion and worldly status

- God always chooses the best person for the Prophetic office, regardless of financial status. Also, material possessions have absolutely no relationship to moral or spiritual guidance.
- If a person is rich in this world, this does not mean in any way that he will be morally strong or that God is pleased with him. Similarly, a person's poverty in this world does not indicate God's anger toward him.
- This life is a test, and God tests people with both abundance and lack of wealth.
- God guides towards the straight path, and He decides whom to bestow His guidance upon.
- God responded to this objection in Surah Zukhruf (full Arabic is omitted)

وَ قَالُوا لَوْ لَا نُزِّلَ هٰذَا الْقُرْاٰنُ   – – – –   وَ الْاٰخِرَةُ عِنْدَ رَبِّکَ لِلْمُتَّقِینَ

And they said: "Why was this Quran not sent down upon a great man from [one of] the two cities?" Do they distribute the mercy of your Lord? It is We who have assigned among them their livelihood in the life of this world and have raised some of them above others in degrees [of riches] that they may make use of one another for service. But the mercy of your Lord is better than whatever they accumulate. Were it not for the fear that all people would become one (nation) in disbelief, We would have made for the disbelievers in the Most Merciful God ceilings out of silver and ladders by which they would climb up, doors for their houses, couches on which to recline, and other ornaments of gold. All these are only the means of enjoyment in this world, but the pious will receive their reward from your Lord in the life hereafter.." (Surah Zukhruf:31-35)

Objection 6 – Love for traditions and culture

- The 'new' religion was challenging their self-constructed traditions and the culture they had invented as custodians of the Kabaah.

- By allowing idols to be placed in the Kabaah, they gained the trust and loyalty of many pagan tribes, thereby achieving religious supremacy in the Arabian Peninsula. The message of Prophet Muhammad could destroy that supremacy, and their central religious authority could be lost forever.

- They also considered angels and jinns to be God's partners; angels were considered God's daughters who should be worshiped like God – the Quran destroyed these false beliefs.

- They used to dismiss the entire concept of the day of judgment – they could not believe that Abu Jahl and Abu Lahab would be held accountable before a higher authority and punished for their sins.

- They invented and added many rites in Hajj, like doing Tawaf nude – the Quran called it an act of Satan.

- They had adopted several religious innovations regarding what was acceptable or not for them to eat. They also used to dedicate a portion of their slaughter to their self-made deities besides God.

- **Conclusion:** The message of Islam was challenging not only their old beliefs but also their leadership status in Arabia. Makkah was the business hub at the time, and they feared a severe blow to their financial situation and worldly benefits.

Quran's Response – Truth vs Tradition

- The Quran stresses that Quraysh should seek the truth and accept it when convinced, rather than remain loyal to their traditions and practices.

وَ اِذَا قِيْلَ لَهُمُ اتَّبِعُوْا مَآ اَنْزَلَ اللّٰهُ قَالُوْا بَلْ نَتَّبِعُ مَآ اَلْفَيْنَا عَلَيْهِ اٰبَآءَنَا ۗ اَوَ لَوْ كَانَ اٰبَآؤُهُمْ لَا يَعْقِلُوْنَ شَيْئًا وَّ لَا يَهْتَدُوْنَ

When they are invited to follow what Allah has revealed, they say, no, we will follow the religion on which we have found our forefathers. Will they do it even if their forefathers did not use their intellect or wisdom, and they were not guided? (Baqarah: 170)

- Prophet Ibrahim deeply hated polytheism, and these practices should never be associated with him. Prophet Ibrahim even reminded his sons of their responsibilities towards the Kabaah in clear terms, one of which was to establish prayers for God alone.

وَ اِذْ قَالَ اِبْرٰهِيْمُ رَبِّ اجْعَلْ هٰذَا الْبَلَدَ اٰمِنًا وَّ اجْنُبْنِيْ وَ بَنِيَّ اَنْ نَّعْبُدَ الْاَصْنَامَ

رَبِّ اِنَّهُنَّ اَضْلَلْنَ كَثِيْرًا مِّنَ النَّاسِ ۚ فَمَنْ تَبِعَنِيْ فَاِنَّهٗ مِنِّيْ ۚ وَ مَنْ عَصَانِيْ فَاِنَّكَ غَفُوْرٌ رَّحِيْمٌ

And remember when Ibrahim said: My Lord, secure this city and keep my sons and me away from worshiping idols. My Lord, indeed, they have led astray many among the people. So, whoever follows me – then he is of me; and whosoever disobeys me – certainly You are yet Forgiving and Merciful (Ibrahim: 35-36)

وَ اذْكُرْ فِي الْكِتٰبِ اِبْرٰهِيْمَ ۚ اِنَّهٗ كَانَ صِدِّيْقًا نَّبِيًّا

اِذْ قَالَ لِاَبِيْهِ يٰاَبَتِ لِمَ تَعْبُدُ مَا لَا يَسْمَعُ وَ لَا يُبْصِرُ وَ لَا يُغْنِيْ عَنْكَ شَيْئًا

And mention in the Book the story of Ibrahim. Indeed, he was a man of truth and a prophet. (And mention) When he said to his father: O my dear father, why do you worship that which does not hear, does not see, and will not benefit you at all? (Maryam:41-42)

- It is unfair to give thanks to anyone other than God when they know they are reaping the benefits of God's blessings.
- Both angels and jinns are the creation of God, and they are aware of their status and responsibilities in God's Universe.
- The Quran also presented compelling arguments for the day of judgment and its essential role in God's scheme for this universe.
- Keeping idols in Kabaah defeats the very purpose of this house, which is built to establish the center of pure monotheism on earth.
- Regarding Halal and Haram, it is the right of God and His Messengers only to declare something as such.

God's law of guidance in the Quran

- Many critics of Islam and the Quran think that when the Quran says that God guides whoever He wills, there is no principle behind it.
- The Quran described this law and principle in detail so we can understand who receives guidance from God.

If you cherish the inner guidance

- One of the tests we all go through is how we react when we face the truth in any aspect of our lives.
- Do we listen carefully, adopt it, and adhere to it, or do we avoid it because of our emotions or because of some other temporary benefits?
- The guidance towards one God and the Hereafter is inner guidance supported by the signs in the heavens and the earth around us.
- If the person cherishes this 'inner' guidance, then God increases in him the desire for guidance, and external guidance, such as that of a prophet or a book like the Quran, also helps.
- In that case, angels and righteous people offer further guidance to the person.

If you neglect the inner guidance

- A person may neglect inner guidance, refuse to use his mind, and deliberately deviate from the truth.
- God shows His signs and warnings, both inside and outside, as reminders.
- If the person persists in disobedience and shows no sign of turning back, God then leaves them to wander in error and misguidance.
- In Quranic terms, that person commits "*Zulm*" (injustice) to himself and is deprived of the ability to think and understand in the proper manner.
- Satan and his agents support this person in everything he does, and he believes he is doing the right thing.

وَ الَّذِيْنَ جَاهَدُوْا فِيْنَا لَنَهْدِيَنَّهُمْ سُبُلَنَا ۚ وَ اِنَّ اللّٰهَ لَمَعَ الْمُحْسِنِيْنَ

[Give glad tidings to My servants, O Prophet:] Those who are bearing difficulties in our path, We shall definitely guide them to Our ways, and undoubtedly God is with those who act with excellence. (29:69)

يُضِلُّ بِهٖ كَثِيْرًا ۙ وَّ يَهْدِىٰ بِهٖ كَثِيْرًا ۚ وَ مَا يُضِلُّ بِهٖ اِلَّا الْفٰسِقِيْنَ

[In this way,] God misleads many by it (Quran), and many He leads to the right path by it; and, in reality, He only misleads by it the rebellious ones. (2:26)

The Guide

- Only Allah guides to the straight path; the Prophets and others are merely means of guidance.
- Guidance must be the most precious thing for a believer. That's why we ask at least 17 times in a day, "Guide us to the straight path," reciting Surah Fatihah in our prayers.
- Guidance to the path of God is the only dua that God does not reject or delay, as guaranteed in the Quran.
- However, while Allah is the ultimate source of guidance, the Quran establishes that a person must take the first step toward the truth to receive it.
- Tawfeeq is a special divine gift in which Allah opens a person's heart to accept and act on the truth.

وَّ لِيَعْلَمَ الَّذِينَ أُوْتُوا الْعِلْمَ اَنَّهُ الْحَقُّ مِنْ رَّبِّكَ فَيُؤْمِنُوْا بِهٖ فَتُخْبِتَ لَهٗ قُلُوْبُهُمْ ۗ وَ اِنَّ اللّٰهَ لَهَادِ الَّذِينَ اٰمَنُوْۤا اِلٰى صِرَاطٍ مُّسْتَقِيْمٍ

And this also happens because those who have been given the knowledge of the Book of God should fully know that the truth has come from your Lord. So, their faith should be strengthened in it, and their hearts bow down before it.[96] And it is God's decision that He shall definitely show the straight path to those who have accepted faith. (22:54)

Is that a sign of anger from Allah if someone is poor and has been deprived of blessings in this world?

SEERAH ACTIVITY

Time to Complete: _____

Instructions: Please print this page and complete it.

SEERAH WORD SEARCH

```
Z P A L E S T I N E
A E A B D U L L A H
I B B X M A K K A H
B T Y Q U R A I S H
R C N S J A M E E N
A M E S S E N G E R
H K H A D I J A H S
I O R P H A N I X J
M O N O T H E I S M
V W M U H A M M A D
```

Monotheism	Palestine	Abyssinia
Messenger	Ibrahim	Makkah
Orphan	Ameen	Muhammad
Abdullah	Khadijah	Quraish

Chapter 17

Seeking help from the People of the Book

Disbelievers from the Quraish tried everything to discredit Prophet Muhammad and his message. In this chapter, we will learn how they sought help from the People of the Book, especially Jews.

Quraysh sought help from the Jews

- Jews settled in Medina and the surrounding area because they believed this was where the last prophet would come. However, they expected the arrival of that prophet within their progeny (children of Israel or Ishaq) because they considered themselves the 'chosen people of God'.

- Jews have always looked at Ishmaelites (their cousins) as their enemies, and any news about a prophet coming among them would not make them happy.

- However, Quraysh sent one of their leaders, Nadr bin Harith, to the Jewish leaders in Medina (Yathrib at the time) to gather information on religion and revelation they could use to counter the attacks on the Quran.

- Up until now, Jews were silent spectators and only occasionally supported the Quraysh (while remaining behind the scenes).

- Quraysh wanted to get the opinion of the people of the book about Prophet Muhammad, knowing that they claimed to receive revelation from God, and also followed prophets from before.

- They also wanted to gather information on the signs they could use to test Prophet Muhammad's claim to prophethood. Only God knows if that was their intent or if they just wanted to discredit Prophet Muhammad and his message, and were looking for excuses.

- At the same time, Jews did not want to openly oppose the Prophet, as the local Arab nationalism could become a challenge in doing so. The local Arabs of Makkah, Medina, and Taif did not like Jews because of their role in the area and their superiority complex.

- The Jews had their own objections that the Quran addressed. They are described in the next section.

- **Jews' plan:** To keep a careful eye on the Prophet and see what he has to say, while indirectly helping the Quraysh fight back against the message.

- Although God had different expectations from them:

وَ اٰمِنُوْا بِمَاۤ اَنْزَلْتُ مُصَدِّقًا لِّمَا مَعَكُمْ وَ لَا تَكُوْنُوْۤا اَوَّلَ كَافِرٍ بِهٖ ۫ وَ لَا تَشْتَرُوْا بِاٰيٰتِیْ ثَمَنًا قَلِیْلًا ۫ وَّ اِیَّاَیَ فَاتَّقُوْنِ

And profess faith in this [Quran] which I have revealed in confirmation of what you already have. And be not the first ones to deny it (among those who already carry the divine book), and do not sell My revelations for a low price, and fear only My wrath. (2:41)

Objection of the Jews

Objection 1 – The Quran being a revelation (Wahi)

- They tried to convince the Quraysh that anyone who claimed revelation from God must be lying because there is no reason for God to send his revelation (Wahi) through a human being.
- It was a deliberate attempt from the Jews to misguide Quraysh - they knew that Prophet Musa was a human being who received Wahi from God.

Quran's Response

- If Musa was given Wahi for guidance, then why could it not be given to Muhammad as well?
- God told them that they had made changes to the original message of God, and many things have been added to religion based on their desires.
- At the same time, Jews were hiding parts of the revelation, following their desires, and hence made it necessary for God to send the final revelation, which cannot be hidden easily.
- God told them that this was in continuation of what they already had from God.

وَ مَا قَدَرُوا اللهَ حَقَّ قَدْرِهٖ اِذْ قَالُوْا مَآ اَنْزَلَ اللهُ عَلٰى بَشَرٍ مِّنْ شَىْءٍ ۙ قُلْ مَنْ اَنْزَلَ الْكِتٰبَ الَّذِىْ جَآءَ بِهٖ مُوْسٰى نُوْرًا وَّ هُدًى لِّلنَّاسِ تَجْعَلُوْنَهٗ قَرَاطِيْسَ تُبْدُوْنَهَا وَ تُخْفُوْنَ كَثِيْرًا ۚ وَ عُلِّمْتُمْ مَّا لَمْ تَعْلَمُوْٓا اَنْتُمْ وَ لَآ اٰبَآؤُكُمْ ۚ قُلِ اللهُ ۙ ثُمَّ ذَرْهُمْ فِيْ خَوْضِهِمْ يَلْعَبُوْنَ

"And they did not give true appreciation to God when they said: "God did not reveal to a human being anything." Say: "Who revealed the Scripture that Musa brought as light and guidance to the people? You [Jews] make it into pages, disclosing some of it and concealing much. And you were taught that which you knew not - neither you nor your fathers." Say: "God [revealed it]." Then leave them in their [empty] discourse, amusing themselves." (Surah Anaam:91)

Objection 2 – Quran is in the Arabic Language

- Jews said all previous scriptures were in Hebrew, so this new one could not be in Arabic. If it were from God, it must be in Hebrew because God does not change His acts. Due to enmity with Arabs and especially with the children of Ismail, they were trying to misguide them as they had shut their eyes to the guidance given to them in their own language, i.e., Torah.

Quran's Response

- The Quran argues that God would reveal a book among Arabs in any other language if they only understood the Arabic language.
- The previous scriptures were sent to a different nation. The guidance to a nation always comes in the language they understand.
- The Quran told them they were looking for excuses to deny it. They would produce another excuse if this book were revealed in a non-Arabic language.

وَ لَوْ جَعَلْنٰهُ قُرْاٰنًا اَعْجَمِيًّا لَّقَالُوْا لَوْ لَا فُصِّلَتْ اٰيٰتُهٗ ؕ ءَاَعْجَمِيٌّ وَّ عَرَبِيٌّ ؕ قُلْ هُوَ لِلَّذِيْنَ اٰمَنُوْا هُدًى وَّ شِفَآءٌ ؕ وَ الَّذِيْنَ لَا يُؤْمِنُوْنَ فِيْٓ اٰذَانِهِمْ وَقْرٌ وَّ هُوَ عَلَيْهِمْ عَمًى ؕ اُولٰٓئِكَ يُنَادَوْنَ مِنْ مَّكَانٍ بَعِيْدٍ

"And if We had made it a non-Arabic Quran, they would have said: 'Why are its verses not explained in detail [in our language]? Is it a foreign [recitation] and an Arab [messenger]?' Say: 'It is a guidance and cure for those who believe.' And those who do not believe – in their ears is deafness, and it is upon them blindness. Those are being called from a distant place." (Surah Fussilat:44)

Objection 3 – Support from the People of the Book

- When they noticed that there was much in common between the teachings of the Quran and the Torah, they claimed that Prophet Muhammad was definitely receiving help from someone within their group.
- Some historians have even named a person they believed helped Prophet Muhammad write the Quran.
- Interestingly, some critics of the Quran today also raise the same objection after doing their so-called 'research'.

Quran's Response

- The Quran is the last divine book of God, not the first. You will find many similar events and facts repeated in the Quran, and in many places, the Quran corrected the facts that the Jews had twisted.
- The people who were living in that area close to the Prophet were all non-Arabs (many of them were Christian slaves), and the Quran is in pure Arabic language; a non-Arab could not produce such a powerful, majestic, and flawless text in the Arabic language.
- The Quran did not blindly follow what was written in the Torah and Bible of that time, but corrected many misconceptions and deviations caused by the Jews.
- The Quran introduced many topics that did not exist in the Torah or the Bible.

وَ لَقَدْ نَعْلَمُ أَنَّهُمْ يَقُولُونَ إِنَّمَا يُعَلِّمُهُ بَشَرٌ ۗ لِسَانُ الَّذِى يُلْحِدُونَ إِلَيْهِ أَعْجَمِىٌّ
وَّ هٰذَا لِسَانٌ عَرَبِىٌّ مُّبِينٌ

And We certainly know that they say: 'It is only a human being who teaches the Prophet.' (Don't they think) The tongue of the one they refer to is foreign, and this Quran is in a clear Arabic language." (Nahl:103)

وَ مَا كُنْتَ تَتْلُوا مِنْ قَبْلِهِ مِنْ كِتَابٍ وَّ لَا تَخُطُّهُ بِيَمِينِكَ إِذًا لَّارْتَابَ الْمُبْطِلُونَ

And you did not recite any scripture before it, nor did you write one with your right hand. Otherwise, the rejectors would have had [cause for] doubt." (Al-Ankabut:48)

Objection 4 – Differences between Quran & other books

- To maintain their leadership role in the area and to continue thinking of themselves as God's 'chosen nation', they did not like the idea of any other divine scripture being given to anyone but them.
- For that, they questioned why they needed another book when there were other divine books. Also, why were the laws given in the Quran different from those given in previous scriptures? Has God changed His mind?

Quran's Response

- Their attitude towards divine books has been rude, and they used to divide them into many parts, hiding some portions from the common people and altering others.
- They used to hide those sections (or lose or change them) that did not suit them.
- As a result, they lost the written Torah entirely, and it was recompiled from memory at a time when it was not customary to memorize scripture.
- The previous scriptures are a combination of the remaining actual words of God and statements/history added by the writers or Jewish/Christian scholars.
- Every nation has been given laws according to its time and circumstances. Since the Quran has been sent for the entirety of humanity, the laws have been changed or reduced to accommodate many societies. There was nothing strange about it.
- Some laws were restored because Jews/Christians had changed them, like Fasting.

$$\text{كَمَا أَنْزَلْنَا عَلَى الْمُقْتَسِمِينَ ۞ الَّذِينَ جَعَلُوا الْقُرْآنَ عِضِينَ}$$

Similarly, we revealed for these dividers (Jews) who used to divide their scripture into sections (Hijr: 90-91)

- The Quran talks about the revelation given to the Jews (their Quran, which is Torah) and calls them dividers, people who divide a divine scripture into sections; some they like and show, and some they don't like and hide.

Objection 5 – Demand for physical miracles

- Their prophets used to demonstrate miracles as proof of their divine message, and every prophet could be identified through his miracles, but this prophet did not show any physical miracles.

Quran's Response

- The Quran recorded their demand for miracles, such as an angel descending from heaven bearing pure, untouched paper bearing the divine message.
- Prophet Musa and many other prophets before him were given amazing miracles, but the nations, including the Jews, still disobeyed their prophets and even killed them after seeing these miracles.
- The miracles were given to the prophet to face the powerful people of their time. E.g., in Egypt, Musa was among those skilled in magic. Prophet Daud and Suleiman were given miracles because they were kings and faced nations with powerful military forces.
- The Quran is itself a living miracle until the day of judgment. Physical miracles are limited to time and space; the Quran was made a miracle for the people of all times and places.

$$\text{وَ لَقَدْ آتَيْنَا مُوسَى تِسْعَ آيَاتٍ بَيِّنَاتٍ فَسْئَلْ بَنِى إِسْرَاءِيلَ إِذْ جَاءَهُمْ فَقَالَ لَهُ فِرْعَوْنُ}$$
$$\text{إِنِّى لَأَظُنُّكَ يَا مُوسَى مَسْحُورًا}$$

And We had certainly given Musa nine evident signs, so ask the Children of Israel [about] when he came to them, and Pharaoh said to him: "Indeed I think, O Musa, that you are affected by the magic." (Israa:101)

$$\text{ذَلِكَ بِأَنَّهُمْ كَانَتْ تَأْتِيهِمْ رُسُلُهُمْ بِالْبَيِّنَاتِ فَكَفَرُوا فَأَخَذَهُمُ اللّٰهُ ۚ إِنَّهُ قَوِيٌّ شَدِيدُ الْعِقَابِ}$$

This happened because their messengers brought clear signs, but they refused to accept them, so Allah punished them. Indeed, He is Powerful and strict in punishing (such people) (Ghafir:22)

Objection 6 – Testing the Prophet for his Prophethood

- They said that if he is a true prophet, he must know, or say, what God told him about incidents that occurred in the past but are not well known in general. They thought the prophet would present fictional statements and try to make up stories about those events, which their scholars would later challenge.
- Only a prophet can tell those stories after receiving their details from God.

Quran's Response

- The Quran answered all the questions they raised in detail across many Surahs and also blamed them for not learning from these stories.
- The Quran also corrected all the wrong beliefs and perspectives associated with those historical events and presented them in their true form.
- The Quran told the believers to know how people before them had struggled in the path of God and clarified some of their own concerns.

Questions posed by the Jews

Q1: Who were Ashab-e-Kahaf?

Q2: Who was Dhul-Qarnain?

Q3: How did the Israelites end up in Egypt?

Q4: What is the nature of *Ruh* or Revelation?

Note: Some historical reports suggest Jews asked more than four questions.

First Question: Ashab-e-Kahaf

- The Quran tells the complete story of the people of the cave, a few young men who God helped in an unusual way in Surah Kahaf.
- Their story became a miracle for the people.
- Jews insisted on their count and how many years they slept, and did not learn any lessons from the story.
- It was also a great story for the Muslims to learn lessons from.

Second Question: The story of Dhul-Qarnain

- Again, this story was told in Surah Kahaf in detail.
- Dhul-Qarnain (Khawras) was the king who built Jerusalem for the Jews.
- Despite being a great conqueror, he strongly believed in God and the Day of Judgment.
- He attributed all his might and success to God.
- He was kind to the people he ruled over and always helped the oppressed.

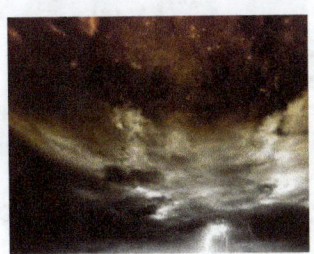

Third Question: What is *Ruh*?

- This was a trick question because Jews themselves didn't know the reality of *Ruh* (revelation) and how it came to a Prophet.
- The Quran clearly states in Surah Bani Israel that only God knows what revelation is, and very little knowledge has been given to human beings about it.

Fourth Question: How did the Israelites end up in Egypt?

- The Quran gave the entire story of the birth of the Israelites in Egypt in Surah Yusuf.
- A caravan took Prophet Yusuf to Egypt after he was taken from the well where his brothers had thrown him.
- He settled there, after which the rest of his family followed.
- The children of Israel were the next generation of these 12 brothers.

Objection 7 – Whose prophet is superior?

- They started this debate that the Israelites and their prophets are better than Prophet Muhammad because many prophets came to them, each with unique attributes and miracles.

- Their initial goal was to create a bias among their own people so they would not listen to the Prophet and the Quran.

- At the same time, they attempted to lower Prophet Muhammad's position in front of the Muslims by saying such things.

- They started talking about the qualities of the Israelites and their prophets, and the lack of such attributes in Prophet Muhammad.

- The idea was to shake the faith of those who had either accepted Islam or were leaning toward it.

Quran's Response

- The Quran made it a part of the Muslim faith to accept and recognize all the prophets of God and declared that Muslims must not compare them with each other, or else they would lose sight of the real goal of the message.

تِلْكَ الرُّسُلُ فَضَّلْنَا بَعْضَهُمْ عَلَى بَعْضٍ ۘ مِنْهُمْ مَّنْ كَلَّمَ اللَّهُ وَ رَفَعَ بَعْضَهُمْ دَرَجَٰتٍ

These are the messengers among them; we made some of them exceed others (in various ways), and among them is the one whom we spoke, and for some, we increased their ranks (Baqarah:253)

وَ رَبُّكَ اَعْلَمُ بِمَنْ فِي السَّمٰوٰتِ وَ الْاَرْضِ ۘ وَ لَقَدْ فَضَّلْنَا بَعْضَ النَّبِيِّنَ عَلَى بَعْضٍ وَّ اٰتَيْنَا دَاوٗدَ زَبُوْرًا

And your Lord knows best of whoever is in the Heavens and the earth. And We have made some prophets exceed others [in various ways], and to David, We gave the book of Psalms." (Israa:55)

Which prophet is the most beloved in the sight of Allah? Think carefully in the light of what you have learned so far.

Objection 8 – Making fun of the Quran

- The Quran has talked about their mischievous behavior when the Jews used to make fun of the teachings of God.
- So, they taught Quraysh also that one way to lower the value of the Quran was to make fun of its verses, especially those they could not comprehend and those related to the next life. They claimed such 'foolish' things could not be said in a divine book. They chose to ridicule the Quran's descriptions of the day of judgment in particular.

Quran's Response

- The description of the unseen world in the Quran has always been a test for the disbelievers and critics of the Quran today.
- The Quran describes Hellfire, stating that these verses will serve as a test for some people. Jews objected to these verses:
  - God had assigned 19 angels to manage Hell (or some part of it).
  - A cactus tree would grow from the base of Hell (within the fire), the fruit of which would be given as food to the people of hell.
- The behavior of the Jews was very surprising. They were familiar with the divine revelations and migrated to this land, waiting for the last prophet. They are familiar with the description of the unseen world in the divine scriptures. The Quran used this opportunity to address the learned and more sincere people among the People of the Book. It brought these events to light with details, allowing them to reflect on and come closer to Islam, which they had previously believed in through the teachings of Prophet Musa.

عَلَيْهَا تِسْعَةَ عَشَرَ

وَ مَا جَعَلْنَا اَصْحٰبَ النَّارِ اِلَّا مَلٰٓئِكَةً ۪ وَّ مَا جَعَلْنَا عِدَّتَهُمْ اِلَّا فِتْنَةً لِّلَّذِينَ كَفَرُوا ۙ لِيَسْتَيْقِنَ الَّذِينَ اُوتُوا الْكِتٰبَ وَ يَزْدَادَ الَّذِينَ اٰمَنُوٓا اِيْمَانًا وَّ لَا يَرْتَابَ الَّذِينَ اُوتُوا الْكِتٰبَ وَ الْمُؤْمِنُوْنَ ۙ وَ لِيَقُوْلَ الَّذِينَ فِيْ قُلُوْبِهِمْ مَّرَضٌ وَّ الْكٰفِرُوْنَ مَاذَآ اَرَادَ اللّٰهُ بِهٰذَا مَثَلًا

"And We have not made the keepers of the Fire except angels. And We have not mentioned their number except as a trial for those who disbelieve - that those who were given the Books will be convinced and those who have believed will increase in faith and those who were given the Books and the believers will not doubt and that those in whose hearts is hypocrisy and the disbelievers will say: 'What does God intend by this as an example?' (74:31)

الْخَبِيرُ

All-Knowing

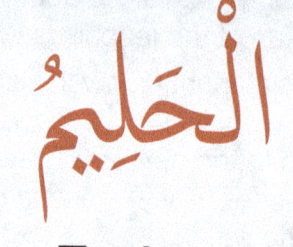

الْحَلِيمُ

The Forbearing

- These two attributes, when considered together, reveal something unique about God.
- The people who deliberately deny God's message or disobey Him openly or in secret must know that God is All-Knowing, and He knows the state of their hearts and minds.
- In the Quran, God has told us that He even knows what's in our hearts and minds before we say or do anything.
- People who make fun of God and the Quran don't realize that they are living on His earth and get all kinds of blessings from Him (food, water, rain, home, etc).
- But then why does He not punish them, since He is very Forbearing at the same time?
- Due to His Forbearance, He continues to give people multiple chances to fix their affairs, and He is ready to forgive when they are willing to come back to Him.
- He overlooks our mistakes and continues to bless us.

لَا يُؤَاخِذُكُمُ اللهُ بِاللَّغْوِ فِي اَيْمَانِكُمْ وَ لٰكِنْ يُؤَاخِذُكُمْ بِمَا كَسَبَتْ قُلُوْبُكُمْ وَ اللهُ غَفُوْرٌ حَلِيْمٌ

God will not hold you liable for your oaths you swear inadvertently. But He shall definitely hold you accountable for oaths sworn with your heart's intent and, in reality, God is Forgiving, very Forbearing. (2:225)

لَا تُدْرِكُهُ الْاَبْصَارُ ۫ وَ هُوَ يُدْرِكُ الْاَبْصَارَ ۚ وَ هُوَ اللَّطِيْفُ الْخَبِيْرُ

God will not hold you liable for your oaths you swear inadvertently. But He shall definitely hold you accountable for oaths sworn with your heart's intent and, in reality, God is Forgiving, very Forbearing. (2:225)

Why must the Quran be in the Arabic language?

What would have happened if a few physical miracles had been given to Prophet Muhammad instead of the Quran?

SEERAH ACTIVITY

STORYTELLING

Select an early Muslim from the list, read their story of conversion to Islam from an authentic source (book or internet), and narrate their story in 1-2 minutes to the class as they would narrate.

- Bilal Ibn Rabah (RA)
- Khabbab Ibn Al-Arat (RA)
- Ammar bin Yasir (RA)
- Omar Ibn Khattab (RA)
- Hamza bin Al-Muttalib (RA)
- Musab Ibn Umair (RA)
- Abu Dhar Ghaffari (RA)

Chapter 18

Economic and Social Boycott

In this chapter, we will talk about the technique that disbelievers used to break the impact of Prophet Muhammad and Islam, and that was the economic and social boycott of the family of Prophet Muhammad and Muslims.

Economic and Social Boycott

The plot to kill the Prophet

- It is said that in the 7th year of Prophethood, all the Quraishi tribes came together and agreed that they should kill Prophet Muhammad.
- But they realize that it will not be easy for Bani Hashim to hand over the Prophet to them.
- They wanted to pay the blood money for the Prophet's life to the Bani Hashim while using other tribes to kill him, so that they could not be avenged.
- They again went to Abu Talib and told him he had little choice. Either he hands over Prophet Muhammad to them, and they will pay the blood money, or they will cut Bani Hashim (a small tribe of Quraish) from Quraish. Bani Hashim won't receive any food or water, and all marriage ties will be cut off.

How did it start?

- After failing to convince Banu Hashim and especially Abu Talib to withdraw their support for Prophet Muhammad, some more emotional people decided to punish the whole tribe for this support by carrying out a social boycott.
- Quraysh demanded that the Banu Hashim withdraw their support for Prophet Muhammad and hand him over to them.
- There are different accounts of the location and nature of this boycott. Some of the details are:
    - **Narration 1:** An agreement was signed among tribes to put Banu Hashim and their ally, Banu Muttalib, under siege in a valley named *Sha'ab Abi Talib*, and Muslims from other tribes were part of the boycott.
    - **Narration 2:** Banu Hashim and Banu Muttalib decided to get together in this valley to show force and support for Prophet Muhammad, and that's how the boycott started, and it was not a siege.
    - **Narration 3:** It was a different valley close to Kabaah where most of the people from Banu Hashim used to live, including Prophet Muhammad and his uncle Abu Talib, and it was not a siege.
    - **Narration 4:** It was a collective agreement among all tribes to boycott Banu Hashim and Banu Muttalib, and it was a complete and severe boycott with no access to even necessary items of food.
    - **Narration 5:** A group of disbelievers from Quraysh, not all, promised each other and wrote an agreement to boycott Banu Hashim. It was a partial boycott, and no agreement was written or signed; some people were against it.

The Boycott

- Quraysh used the boycott as one of the ways to stop the message of Islam since they had realized the power of this message and how it could affect their leadership position.
- Some Muslims, like Abu Bakr and Omar, were not affected as a result of this boycott, which suggests that it was not a siege, or else Omar would not have tolerated this behavior from the Quraysh.
- The boycott involved:
  - Ending all trade relations and developing none with them.
  - Not developing new relationships through marriages – no one would marry the daughters of Banu Hashim.
  - Restricting social activities and not sharing food and other items as they used to before.
  - Isolating Banu Hashim and Banu Muttalib to the extent that they would feel worried and remain under pressure to pay attention to the demands of the Quraysh.
- Prophet Muhammad and his companions were still allowed to move freely in the land, and as a result, the work of spreading Islam's message never stopped.
- Banu Hashim could trade with others who were not part of the agreement or who chose to participate in the boycott; it is reported that some elders opposed this approach, and that's what ended it.

Attempts to Compromise

- Quraysh realized that their oppression was not hurting the message but, instead, was hurting their position in Arabia because of the sufferings that children and women went through as a consequence of this oppression.
- They produced a more compromising proposal that would allow them to accept the message:
  - Prophet Muhammad should 'adjust' some parts of his teachings.
  - Some people couldn't abandon certain practices, so he should let them do what they were doing.
- Prophet Muhammad was a well-wisher of his people. He began thinking about their proposal and weighed the pros and cons of the flexibility Quraysh was requesting.

- Quraysh even tried to convince Prophet Muhammad, through Abu Talib, to accept their proposal.
- In clear terms, the Quran forbade the Prophet Muhammad from even considering it and instructed him not to compromise under any circumstances.
- Quranic verses revealed to him that when a Prophet comes with a message, he is not allowed to change according to the circumstances or on his own.

وَ اِنْ كَادُوا لَيَفْتِنُوْنَكَ عَنِ الَّذِيْٓ اَوْحَيْنَآ اِلَيْكَ لِتَفْتَرِىَ عَلَيْنَا غَيْرَهٗ ۖ وَ اِذًا لَّاتَّخَذُوْكَ خَلِيْلًا

وَ لَوْ لَآ اَنْ ثَبَّتْنٰكَ لَقَدْ كِدْتَّ تَرْكَنُ اِلَيْهِمْ شَيْئًا قَلِيْلًا

اِذًا لَّاَذَقْنٰكَ ضِعْفَ الْحَيٰوةِ وَ ضِعْفَ الْمَمَاتِ ثُمَّ لَا تَجِدُ لَكَ عَلَيْنَا نَصِيْرًا

And indeed, they were about to tempt you away from what We revealed to you to [make] you invent something else about Us, and then they would have taken you as a friend. And if We had not strengthened you, you would have almost inclined to them a little. Then, if you had, we would have made you taste double punishment in life and double after death. Then you would not find a helper for yourself against us." (Bani Israel:73-75)

وَ اِذَا تُتْلٰى عَلَيْهِمْ اٰيَاتُنَا بَيِّنٰتٍ ۙ قَالَ الَّذِيْنَ لَا يَرْجُوْنَ لِقَآءَنَا ائْتِ بِقُرْاٰنٍ غَيْرِ هٰذَآ اَوْ بَدِّلْهُ ؕ قُلْ مَا يَكُوْنُ لِيْٓ اَنْ اُبَدِّلَهٗ مِنْ تِلْقَآئِ نَفْسِيْ ۚ اِنْ اَتَّبِعُ اِلَّا مَا يُوْحٰى اِلَيَّ ۚ اِنِّيْٓ اَخَافُ اِنْ عَصَيْتُ رَبِّيْ عَذَابَ يَوْمٍ عَظِيْمٍ

And when Our verses are recited to them as clear evidence, those who do not expect the meeting with Us say: "Bring us a Quran other than this or change it." Say, "It is not for me to change it on my own accord. I only follow what is revealed to me. Indeed, I fear that if I should disobey my Lord, I will be punished on a tremendous day. (Yunus: 15)

- In summary, the intent of the Quraysh from this boycott was to pressure the Banu Hashim to remove their protection from the Prophet Muhammad, so they could take extreme action to kill the Prophet.
- Abu Talib, his guardian in the early days, did not allow this to happen and supported the Prophet despite the economic and social challenges his family and tribe faced as a result.
- It is reported that the boycott lasted almost three years, and many families suffered financially and emotionally. The Prophet, his family, and companions faced such harsh conditions yet never compromised on the true message of Islam.

Abu Bakr wanted to Migrate

- Abu Bakr was highly respected among the Quraysh. He was a very patient and honorable person.
- But even such a steadfast person felt annoyed by the brutal behavior of the Quraysh and decided to migrate to Abyssinia.
- Abu Bakr met his friend Bin al-Daghnah and told him he was leaving Makkah to worship God in a free environment.
- Al-Daghnah told him to stay and gave him his protection as the leader of the tribe, Qarrah.
- He met all the leaders of the Quraysh and told them that a kind person like Abu Bakr should never leave Makkah since he is someone who "helps the poor, treats his relatives well, carries the burdens of others, takes care of guests, and supports them".
- Quraysh accepted Al-Dahnah's protection and allowed Abu Bakr to pray and read the Quran in his house, and not in public.
- Abu Bakr used to read the Quran with a soft voice and cry while reading, attracting many passers-by to the Quran. Quraysh complained to al-Daghnah about it, and al-Daghnah asked Abu Bakr to avoid doing so so that he could continue providing his protection.
- Abu Bakr refused to comply and refused his protection, saying that he was happy with the protection of God and decided not to migrate anymore and fight the oppression of the Quraysh.

What is the impact of social and economic boycott on the affected in a tribal society?

The Provider

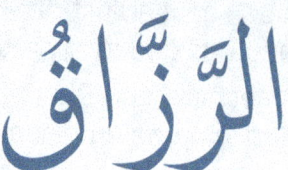

- God gives us even those things that our parents or siblings give us, and He is the ultimate Provider of everything.
- Rizq has been given to us for our benefit, including our parents, money, clothes, family, home, time, etc.
- God is Ar-Razzaq because He not only provides for us once but takes care of us through our entire lives, without any gap in between
- He provides for us, animals, and plants, all at the same time
- When it comes to our sustenance or Rizq, we should make our best effort and then have faith in Him that He will provide for us because He is already providing for us many things without asking

وَ مَا مِنْ دَآبَّةٍ فِي الْأَرْضِ اِلَّا عَلَى اللهِ رِزْقُهَا وَ يَعْلَمُ مُسْتَقَرَّهَا وَ مُسْتَوْدَعَهَا ۚ كُلٌّ فِي كِتَبٍ مُّبِينٍ

And there is no creature on earth, but that upon Allah is its provision [Rizq], and He knows its place of dwelling and place of storage. All is in a clear book (with us)." (Hud: 6)

وَ مَا خَلَقْتُ الْجِنَّ وَ الْاِنْسَ اِلَّا لِيَعْبُدُونِ ۚ مَآ اُرِيْدُ مِنْهُمْ مِّنْ رِّزْقٍ وَّ مَآ اُرِيْدُ اَنْ يُّطْعِمُونِ

اِنَّ اللهَ هُوَ الرَّزَّاقُ ذُو الْقُوَّةِ الْمَتِيْنُ

I have created the jinn and men only for My worship [and this is what is required of them as well]. I seek no sustenance from them, nor do I want that they should feed me. God Himself is the Provider, the Almighty, and the extremely Powerful. (51:56-58)

HANDWRITE A LETTER

"Handwrite a Letter" to Prophet Muhammad (SAW) and his tribe when they were going through the Boycott.

Instructions

- Be Respectful.
- The letter should <u>not</u> be typed on a computer.
- The letter should be between 300 and 500 words (not more than a standard-sized page).

Chapter 19

Conclusion of the Argument

In this chapter, we will discuss how Prophet Muhammad presented his final arguments to Quraish before God told him to move on to the next stage of preaching: migration.

God's Law of Divine Punishment

- A Messenger is a blessing for a nation, and he delivers his message in the language of the nation.

- The message is given in the most precise terms, in such a way that one can't deny its truth unless he/she has other personal motives that he/she prefer over the truth.

divine = something related to God

- If people have understood the message and rejected it because of their interests, only God can determine it.

- God rules the world. If a nation denies His message and messenger for no good reason and tries to fight against it, then this act is considered a disobedient act against God.

- In this case, the nation deserves God's punishment.

- A time period is given to the nation during which they are free to understand the message, ask questions, and either accept or reject it.

- Everyone is free to accept/reject the message before the punishment is announced.

وَ اِنْ مِّنْ قَرْيَةٍ اِلَّا نَحْنُ مُهْلِكُوْهَا قَبْلَ يَوْمِ الْقِيٰمَةِ اَوْ مُعَذِّبُوْهَا عَذَابًا شَدِيْدًا ۚ كَانَ ذٰلِكَ فِى الْكِتٰبِ مَسْطُوْرًا

There is no town on this earth that we will not bring down (due to bad morals) or destroy (due to rejecting a messenger) before the day of judgment, and it is written in the book of God. (Israa: 58)

The Law

- When a messenger (Rasool) is sent, God decides the fate of that nation before the messenger leaves the nation.

- In the Quran, the different phases (periods) of this law in the life of the Prophet Muhammad, who was sent as a messenger, are captured.

- The following slide summarizes the phases of this law.

Multiple phases of the Law

- God implemented the exact law with the nation of the Prophet Muhammad.

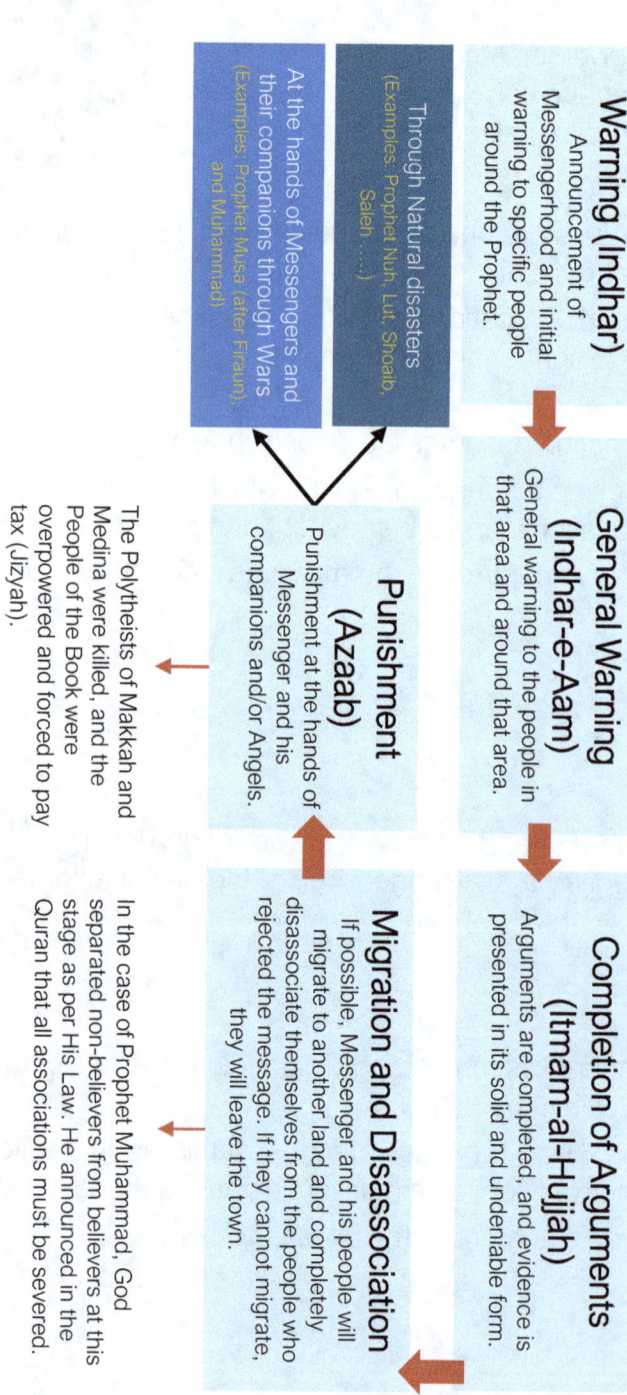

Warning (Indhar)
Announcement of Messengerhood and initial warning to specific people around the Prophet.

Through Natural disasters (Examples: Prophet Nuh, Lut, Shoaib, Saleh ......)

At the hands of Messengers and their companions through Wars (Examples: Prophet Musa (after Firaun), and Muhammad)

General Warning (Indhar-e-Aam)
General warning to the people in that area and around that area.

Completion of Arguments (Itmam-al-Hujjah)
Arguments are completed, and evidence is presented in its solid and undeniable form.

Migration and Disassociation
If possible, Messenger and his people will migrate to another land and completely disassociate themselves from the people who rejected the message. If they cannot migrate, they will leave the town.

In the case of Prophet Muhammad, God separated non-believers from believers at this stage as per His Law. He announced in the Quran that all associations must be severed.

Punishment (Azaab)
Punishment at the hands of Messenger and his companions and/or Angels.

The Polytheists of Makkah and Medina were killed, and the People of the Book were overpowered and forced to pay tax (Jizyah)..

Reasons for physical punishment in this world

- It provides physical proof to those present at that place and time that God's existence is not a fairy tale and that He controls the affairs of this world.
- The event is used as proof that God will reward and punish people on the day of judgment based on their beliefs and actions, just as He has done with this nation in front of their eyes. It acts as a warning for the people to come.

Trials for the people of Makkah

- Before the final punishment comes, God inflicts the nation with various trials to prompt them to heed the message, so that they can humble themselves before God and turn towards Him. It is usually in good times that people become arrogant and refuse to listen to God.
- Elsewhere, God told the Quraysh that they would continue to face trials and difficulties until the final phase of the message was reached, after which the punishment would come.
- This happened at the time of Musa also, and his nation and the Pharaoh's nation were tested with many trials and difficulties.
- It is recorded that Quraysh also suffered through severe famine and trade losses as a sign.

وَ لَا يَزَالُ الَّذِينَ كَفَرُوا تُصِيبُهُمْ بِمَا صَنَعُوا قَارِعَةٌ اَوْ تَحُلُّ قَرِيبًا مِّنْ دَارِهِمْ حَتّٰى يَأْتِيَ وَعْدُ اللهِ ۚ اِنَّ اللهَ لَا يُخْلِفُ الْمِيْعَادَ

And those who disbelieve do not cease to be struck, for what they have done, by calamity – or it will descend near their home – until the promise of God (punishment) comes. Indeed, God does not fail in [His] promise." (Raad:31)

وَ مَآ اَرْسَلْنَا فِيْ قَرْيَةٍ مِّنْ نَّبِيٍّ اِلَّا اَخَذْنَآ اَهْلَهَا بِالْبَأْسَآءِ وَ الضَّرَّآءِ لَعَلَّهُمْ يَضَّرَّعُوْنَ

And We sent to no city a prophet [who was denied], except that We seized its people with poverty and hardship that they might humble themselves [to God]. (Aaraf:94)

Why did God occasionally punish nations on this earth when all acts will be judged on the Day of Judgment?

Warnings to Quraysh

- Despite the trials that the people of Makkah suffered, the Quraysh arrogantly asked Prophet Muhammad to bring down the punishment on them and insisted on asking when it would come – God responded that the knowledge was only with Him.

- With tender feelings in his heart for his nation, the Prophet grew concerned about his people's stubbornness and wondered whether it was his fault that they were not accepting the message.

- In some verses, the Quran indicates that it would be the Prophet and his companions who would punish the disbelievers in a battle, unlike punishments for previous nations, which appeared as natural disasters.

- In Surah Qamar, God first recounted the stories of previous nations, then told Quraysh that they were no different from those nations and would meet the same fate. This was a clear indication that the nation of Prophet Muhammad will face the same consequences.

- The threats of punishment became severe with time. It was predicted that a group of Quraysh leaders would be killed as part of the punishment decreed by God and that there would be several such punishments.

- The influence of the Quraysh was minimal outside of Makkah. That is why the tribes outside Makkah were more receptive to Islam's message. The circle around Quraysh was getting tighter.

- The leaders of Quraysh were confused that, with all their riches and high status in society, it was possible that they could be punished and defeated by just a few people who were weak and had no status in society (they did not realize that Islam was accepted more outside of Makkah).

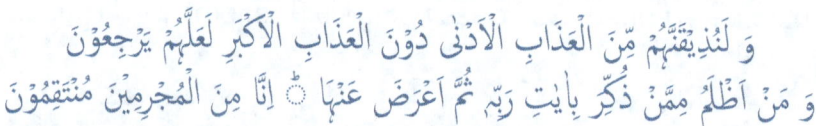

وَ لَنُذِيقَنَّهُمْ مِّنَ الْعَذَابِ الْأَدْنَى دُونَ الْعَذَابِ الْأَكْبَرِ لَعَلَّهُمْ يَرْجِعُونَ

وَ مَنْ أَظْلَمُ مِمَّنْ ذُكِّرَ بِآيَتِ رَبِّهِ ثُمَّ أَعْرَضَ عَنْهَا ۚ إِنَّا مِنَ الْمُجْرِمِينَ مُنْتَقِمُونَ

And we will surely let them taste the nearer punishment (through war) before the greater punishment that may befall them, so that they may repent. And who is more unjust than one who is reminded of the verses of his Lord, then he turns away from them? Indeed, We, from the criminals, will take retribution." (32:21-22)

Verses related to threat for punishment

وَ اِمَّا نُرِيَنَّكَ بَعْضَ الَّذِىْ نَعِدُهُمْ اَوْ نَتَوَفَّيَنَّكَ فَاِلَيْنَا مَرْجِعُهُمْ ثُمَّ اللّٰهُ شَهِيْدٌ عَلٰى مَا يَفْعَلُوْنَ

وَ لِكُلِّ اُمَّةٍ رَّسُوْلٌ ۚ فَاِذَا جَآءَ رَسُوْلُهُمْ قُضِىَ بَيْنَهُمْ بِالْقِسْطِ وَ هُمْ لَا يُظْلَمُوْنَ

وَ يَقُوْلُوْنَ مَتٰى هٰذَا الْوَعْدُ اِنْ كُنْتُمْ صٰدِقِيْنَ

قُلْ لَّاۤ اَمْلِكُ لِنَفْسِىْ ضَرًّا وَّ لَا نَفْعًا اِلَّا مَا شَآءَ اللّٰهُ ؕ لِكُلِّ اُمَّةٍ اَجَلٌ ؕ اِذَا جَآءَ اَجَلُهُمْ فَلَا يَسْتَأْخِرُوْنَ سَاعَةً وَّ لَا يَسْتَقْدِمُوْنَ

قُلْ اَرَءَيْتُمْ اِنْ اَتٰىكُمْ عَذَابُهٗ بَيَاتًا اَوْ نَهَارًا مَّاذَا يَسْتَعْجِلُ مِنْهُ الْمُجْرِمُوْنَ

"And whether We show you some of what We promise them, [O Muhammad], or We take you in death, to Us is their return; then, [either way], God is a witness concerning what they are doing. And for every nation is a messenger. So, when their messenger comes, it will be judged between them in justice, and they will not be wronged. And they say, "When is [the fulfillment of] this promise if you should be truthful?" Say, "I possess no harm or benefit for myself except what God wills for me. For every nation, it is a [specified] term. When their time has come, they will not remain behind an hour, nor will they precede [it]." Say, "Have you considered that if His punishment should come to you by night or day, then what is making these criminals so impatient about it?" (Younus:46-50)

اَكُفَّارُكُمْ خَيْرٌ مِّنْ اُولٰٓئِكُمْ اَمْ لَكُمْ بَرَآءَةٌ فِى الزُّبُرِ ۚ اَمْ يَقُوْلُوْنَ نَحْنُ جَمِيْعٌ مُّنْتَصِرٌ

سَيُهْزَمُ الْجَمْعُ وَ يُوَلُّوْنَ الدُّبُرَ

(After talking about many previous nations, God said) (O Muhammad), Are your disbelievers better than those [former ones], or have you got any protection in the scripture? Or do they say, "We are a powerful assembly supporting [each other]"? [Their] assembly will be defeated, and they will turn their backs [in retreat]. But (besides this punishment) the Hour is their appointment [for due punishment], and the Hour is more disastrous and more bitter." (Qamar:43-46)

Can we warn people around us who are not accepting Islam about similar punishment from God?

Demands for a sign of punishment

- Arrogant people usually take threats against them as an insult, even if they come from God. Quraysh started demanding a sign (or proof) of this punishment.
- The Quran emphasizes that a time has been set for punishment. God would continue to send verses of the Quran that proved its truth, so most of the people of that nation could hear it and had time to ponder and accept it.
- The Prophet was in no position to provide signs of punishment.
- Deep in his heart, the Prophet wished that God would show them a physical sign that would bring his nation to its knees.

Signs of God are all around us

- In response to the constant demands for signs by the Quraysh, the Quran pointed out that people should look within themselves and around:
  - This universe, the birth of human beings, never-ending skies, the earth, valleys, animals, birds, the entire ecosystem, food chain, rain, clouds, and oceans are all signs of the one God who made this all with a perfect balance.
- If people are paying attention to these signs and reflecting on them, they must convey a powerful message that helps us understand the oneness of God and His unique attributes as a Creator.

The sign of the splitting of the moon

- God also gave a majestic sign of His great power during the time of the Prophet.
- He asked the people to look at the moon, and they saw it split into two, with one piece moving towards the front of Mount Nur and the other towards the back.

- It was not something that Prophet Muhammad did. Instead, God did it, and the Prophet only asked people to witness it.
- There are reports in history of some people traveling toward Makkah who also witnessed it and reported it to others when they reached Makkah.

اِقْتَرَبَتِ السَّاعَةُ وَ انْشَقَّ الْقَمَرُ ۝ وَ اِنْ يَّرَوْا اٰيَةً يُّعْرِضُوْا وَ يَقُوْلُوْا سِحْرٌ مُّسْتَمِرٌّ

وَ كَذَّبُوْا وَ اتَّبَعُوْا اَهْوَآءَهُمْ وَ كُلُّ اَمْرٍ مُّسْتَقِرٌّ

The Hour has come near, and the moon has split [into two]. And if they see a miracle (like this), they turn away and say, "This is magic that has occurred before." And they denied and followed their desires. (And wait) for every matter has a [time of] settlement. (Qamar:1-3)

The Prophet's worries

- Being a kind-hearted person, the Prophet was concerned about these threats because he knew that God's punishment would befall them if they did not pay heed.
- When the angel used to come to deliver the message, he would try to get it and memorize it as quickly as possible.
- God told him not to show impatience; that revelation would come when needed, in its allotted time.
- God told him that angels do not come without His permission.

فَتَعٰلَى اللهُ الْمَلِكُ الْحَقُّ ۝ وَ لَا تَعْجَلْ بِالْقُرْاٰنِ مِنْ قَبْلِ اَنْ يُّقْضٰى

اِلَيْكَ وَحْيُهٗ ۝ وَ قُلْ رَّبِّ زِدْنِيْ عِلْمًا

So high [above all] is God, the Sovereign, the Truth. And, [O Muhammad], do not hasten with [recitation of] the Quran before its revelation is completed to you, and say, "My Lord, increase me in knowledge." (Taha:114)

Why do most people ask for physical miracles or signs from the Messengers?

Attention towards the Muslims

- God also told the Prophet to take comfort in the presence of those who have accepted Islam, those who love him dearly. He advised Prophet Muhammad to ignore the disbelievers (after a specific time).
- Allah told the Prophet to continue giving people the message and to read them the new verses of the Quran, but not to consume himself with worry, since his responsibility was to deliver.
- The prophet also had the responsibility of training the believers in Islam, answering their queries, giving them good news for their steadfastness, and helping them achieve closeness to God.

وَ لَا تَطْرُدِ الَّذِيْنَ يَدْعُوْنَ رَبَّهُمْ بِالْغَدٰوةِ وَ الْعَشِيِّ يُرِيْدُوْنَ وَجْهَهٗ مَا عَلَيْكَ مِنْ حِسَابِهِمْ مِّنْ شَيْءٍ وَّ مَا مِنْ حِسَابِكَ عَلَيْهِمْ مِّنْ شَيْءٍ فَتَطْرُدَهُمْ فَتَكُوْنَ مِنَ الظّٰلِمِيْنَ

(O Muhammad, due to your worry about the disbelievers), do not repel (send away) those who call upon their Lord morning and afternoon, seeking His approval. (O Muhammad) Not upon you is anything of their (disbelievers) account, and not upon them is anything of your account. So were you to send them away, you would [then] be one of the wrongdoers. (Anaam:52)

لَا تَمُدَّنَّ عَيْنَيْكَ اِلٰى مَا مَتَّعْنَا بِهٖ اَزْوَاجًا مِّنْهُمْ وَ لَا تَحْزَنْ عَلَيْهِمْ وَ اخْفِضْ جَنَاحَكَ لِلْمُؤْمِنِيْنَ

Do not extend your eyes toward that by which We have given enjoyment to [certain] groups of the disbelievers, and do not grieve over them. And lower your wing to the believers. (Hijr:88)

Incident of Abdullah bin Umm Maktum

عَبَسَ وَ تَوَلّٰى اَنْ جَآءَهُ الْاَعْمٰى وَ مَا يُدْرِيْكَ لَعَلَّهٗ يَزَّكّٰى اَوْ يَذَّكَّرُ فَتَنْفَعَهُ الذِّكْرٰى اَمَّا مَنِ اسْتَغْنٰى فَاَنْتَ لَهٗ تَصَدّٰى وَ مَا عَلَيْكَ اَلَّا يَزَّكّٰى وَ اَمَّا مَنْ جَآءَكَ يَسْعٰى وَ هُوَ يَخْشٰى فَاَنْتَ عَنْهُ تَلَهّٰى

The Prophet frowned and turned away. Because there came to him the blind man, [interrupting his talk with the disbelievers]. But what would make you perceive, [O Muhammad], that perhaps he might be purified? Or be reminded, and the remembrance would benefit him? As for he who thinks himself self-sufficient, To him, you give attention. And not upon you [is any blame] if he will not be purified. But as for he who came to you striving [for knowledge], while he fears [God], from him, you are distracted. (Surah Abasa)

- The prophet was speaking to a group of disbelievers from Quraysh about the Quran when a blind companion, Abdullah bin Umm Maktum (Khadijah's cousin), asked the prophet for permission to enter.
- His interruption displeased Prophet Muhammad, as he did not want to miss any opportunity to convince the Quraysh leaders to save them from the punishment of God.
- Although the Prophet's intention was good, God was displeased with this attitude and communicated His displeasure in the Quran.
- God's anger was actually directed towards the disbelievers who think they are self-sufficient and do not need any guidance.

An unfortunate behavior

- It is a matter of great misfortune for a nation when a prophet who is sincere to them comes among them, giving them the message that would take them from the darkness of ignorance to the light of knowledge, but they refuse to listen to him and obey him for their temporary worldly benefits.
- It is even worse when they fight against God by openly opposing his prophet. In such a situation, these people convert a huge divine favor into great suffering for themselves in the form of punishment.
- Their carelessness and disregard for God, who is their Creator and Ruler, and for His message, is considered an act of rebellion against God. Such rebellious nations cannot escape the consequences of their behavior.
- When nations ignore this message, it is the responsibility of the Prophet to warn them of the negative consequences of their stubbornness and opposition. In this process, God gives the people enough time before He decides the final punishment.

What were the reasons that kept the disbelievers from believing in the message of Islam even after hearing about the punishment?

The Reckoner
The Sufficient

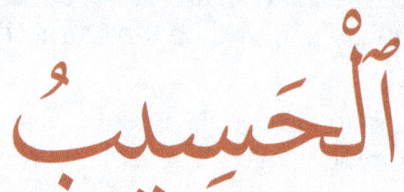

- This name has two shades:
  - For wrongdoers, it signifies God's attribute of keeping an accurate account of all deeds, so they must watch their deeds and not transgress. It is a warning/threat. For believers and everyone, it provides a sense of comfort that He is watching all their good deeds and nothing will be wasted.
  - Secondly, He provides everything needed for His creation and is sufficient for them, which also gives a sense of comfort.
- In general, it reminds us that Allah tracks every action and will hold everyone accountable on the Day of Judgement, while also assuring His servants that He is enough to provide for all their needs, both worldly and spiritual.
- The Quran wants us to be watchful of our deeds and not take any small good or bad deed lightly.

وَكُلَّ اِنْسَانٍ اَلْزَمْنٰهُ طَٰٓئِرَهٗ فِیْ عُنُقِهٖ ۗ وَ نُخْرِجُ لَهٗ یَوْمَ الْقِیٰمَةِ كِتٰبًا یَّلْقٰهُ مَنْشُوْرًا
اِقْرَأْ كِتٰبَكَ ۗ كَفٰی بِنَفْسِكَ الْیَوْمَ عَلَیْكَ حَسِیْبًا

[By relying on their deities, they should not hastily demand the torment.] We have tied the fate of each person with his neck, and on the Day of Judgement, We shall bring forth a register for him which he will find open right before him. Here it is. "Read your account of deeds. Today you yourself are sufficient to take your own account." (17:13-14)

Chapter 20

The Year of Sorrow

In this chapter, we will study what historians called "*Aam Al-Huzn*," the Year of Sorrow, during which the Prophet faced multiple difficult situations.

Most Difficult Year in Prophet's Life

In the year 619 AD, multiple tragedies (sad losses) happened in the life of Prophet Muhammad when both the Prophet's uncle and his wife died. This year was called the "Aam al-Huzn / Year of Sorrow" because of the significant losses he suffered. He also witnessed the worst behavior from the people of Taif.

| He lost his dear uncle. | He lost his dear wife, Khadijah. | The people of Taif tortured him. |

The death of Abu Talib

- The prophet's uncle, Abu Talib, played a critical role in his life. He took care of him when he was young and an orphan, and then he gave his complete protection on behalf of his tribe against the persecution of Quraysh.

- Even though he had a very close bond with his nephew, the Prophet Muhammad, the Prophet's teachings did not change Abu Talib's love for the religion of his forefathers.

- A famous incident is reported when the Prophet visited him on his deathbed. The prophet asked his uncle to accept Islam because God gives a person a chance to repent until their last moment. Abu Jahal and other leaders continued to pressure him by saying, "Would you turn away in the last moment from Abdul Muttalib's religion?"

- Abu Jahal took the leadership of the Prophet's tribe after Abu Talib and increased the oppression and harassment of the Prophet manifold.

The death of Khadijah

- Khadijah also died either a few days or a couple of months after Abu Talib died (as per different reports)

- After her death, the Prophet continued to remember and speak of her qualities and sacrifices for a long time, so much so that the later wives of Prophet Muhammad felt that and expressed it.

Aisha (RA) reported: "I never felt so jealous about any woman as I did for Khadijah. She had died three years before I married the Prophet. I heard him mention her so often, and his Lord ordered him to give her glad tidings of her palace in Paradise, made of reeds. The Prophet would slaughter a sheep and distribute its meat among her friends. (Sahih Al-Bukhari 5658)

- Her death was a great tragedy for the prophet for the following reasons:
  - She was a great moral and financial supporter of Islam and her husband in those difficult times.
  - She witnessed his Prophethood, was the first person to believe in him, and always encouraged him to continue preaching the message of Islam.
  - Khadijah spent her wealth generously for the sake of Islam.
  - Due to her generous support, the Prophet was able to devote all his time to the duties God had given him, without having to worry about earning a living.
  - Prophet Muhammad had six children with Khadijah, including four daughters.
  - She gave so much to the Prophet and became his close companion and partner to the extent that she remained his only wife until her death – in Arab society, multiple marriages were quite common.

Trust in God's support

- The Prophet did not leave his home for many days as he was uncertain how the leaders of the Quraysh would behave after he lost Abu Talib's protection.
- Some people even threw filth (the remains/entrails of a dead camel) on his back once when making sajdah while praying in the Kabaah. People laughed and made fun of him until his daughter, Fatimah, a young girl at that time, afraid of the situation, came and removed the filth from him.
- No matter what, though, the source of his courageous determination in the face of all the painful experiences he had was his strong faith in God and his unshakeable trust in Him.

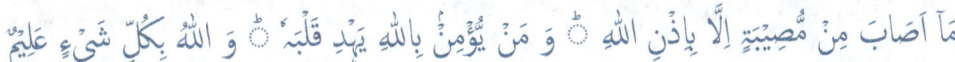

(Remember), No calamity strikes you except by the permission of God, and whosoever believes in God, He will guide his heart (more), and God is fully aware of all things. (Taghabun:11)

The Journey to Taif

- After the Prophet lost the support of Banu Hashim under the new leadership, he decided to seek an alternative place that could offer him protection with God's help.
- Taif and Makkah were considered twin cities because leaders of both cities, known and respected figures throughout the Arab region, frequently traveled between the cities, owned property in each other's cities, and married into each other's families.

- The Prophet approached three influential lords in Taif, all of whom not only refused to accept his teachings but also ridiculed them, saying that they were far away from the religion of their forefathers.
- They also instructed their slaves and children to chase the Prophet out of the city and harass him, eventually causing him injury.
- On his way back from Taif, the Prophet stopped at one of the vineyards belonging to a family in Makkah, who sent him grapes through their slave, Adas.
- Adas found it strange when he heard the Prophet saying "Bismillah". He told the Prophet that he was from the city of Nineveh. The Prophet said that that was the place where "my brother Prophet Younus preached." Upon hearing this, Adas immediately accepted Islam.

A Prophet of Mercy

- The Prophet felt sorrow because of the behavior of the leaders of Taif, and he prayed to God sadly:

"O God, I am weak; my resources are limited, and my efforts are weak. You are the Master of the weak. I have no trust in anyone but You. You will give victory."

- It is reported that at that time, an angel appeared and sought permission from him to crush the city of Taif between two mountains.
- The Prophet stopped him and said that he hoped God would bring forth from the progeny of these cruel individuals those who would worship only one God and pay heed to the true message of God.

Prophet's wife, Aisha, asked Prophet one time: "Was there any day more difficult to you than the Day of Uhud?" The Prophet said, "Yes. Indeed, your people have hurt me a lot. And the worst I got was on the Day of Aqaba (meaning the Incident of Ta'if). (Sahih Bukhari #3231)

There is a debate among Muslims about whether the Prophet's uncle, Abu Talib, accepted Islam on his deathbed and whether he got to paradise or not. What should be our attitude in such matters?

Immediate Relief from God

When prophets are going through difficult times, God allows them to experience something that brings peace and comfort to their hearts (see many examples in the Quran). Something similar happened on the way back from Taif.

Conversation with Addas

- The Prophet did not know that the wall where the Prophet made the dua belonged to Utbah and Shaybah, his distant uncles.
- The two had seen from a distance the Prophet being stoned out of Ta'if, so they felt pity for him and decided to gift him some of their fruits. For that, they sent their servant Addas, an Iraqi Christian, with a bowl of grapes to him.
- The Prophet accepted the gift, said "Bismillah," and began eating.
- Addas was shocked and said, "What is this phrase 'Bismillah'? (This is not the phrase of the local Arabs!)."
- The Prophet said, "This is something my Lord has taught me. And where are you from, O Addas?"
- Addas said, "I am from Nineveh."
- The Prophet smiled and said, "The city of Yunus ibn Matta (Jonah the son of Matthew)?"
- Addas was shocked and said, "How did you know Yunus ibn Matta? Nobody in this whole land has ever heard of him!"
- The Prophet said, "How do I not know Yunus? He is my brother, and I am his brother. We are both prophets of Allah."
- Addas immediately accepted Islam.

Jinns listening to the Quran

- In the area of Nakhlah, the Prophet was reciting the Quran loudly during the night prayers when a group of Jinns passed by and heard the Quran.
- When they reached their community, they informed them that they had heard a great message about the oneness of God after Prophet Musa.
- They said some of them used to sit in the sky, trying to intercept conversations among the angels (about instructions God had given them), but that this is not possible, and now they know why. It is because of this new revelation coming down from the heavens.
- This incident is recorded in Surah Jinn in the Quran.

$$\text{قُلْ أُوحِىَ اِلَىَّ اَنَّهُ اسْتَمَعَ نَفَرٌ مِّنَ الْجِنِّ فَقَالُوٓا اِنَّا سَمِعْنَا قُرْاٰنًا عَجَبًا}$$

$$\text{يَّهْدِىٓ اِلَى الرُّشْدِ فَاٰمَنَّا بِهٖ ۖ وَ لَنْ نُّشْرِكَ بِرَبِّنَآ اَحَدًا}$$

Say, O Muhammad: It has been revealed to me that a group of Jinns listened, and they said: Surely, we have heard a wonderful Quran, which guides us to the right way, so we believe in it, and now we will never set up any partners with Him, ever. (Jinn: 1-2)

$$\text{وَّ اَنَّا لَمَسْنَا السَّمَآءَ فَوَجَدْنٰهَا مُلِئَتْ حَرَسًا شَدِيْدًا وَّ شُهُبًا ۙ}$$

$$\text{وَّ اَنَّا كُنَّا نَقْعُدُ مِنْهَا مَقَاعِدَ لِلسَّمْعِ ۖ فَمَنْ يَّسْتَمِعِ الْاٰنَ يَجِدْ لَهٗ شِهَابًا رَّصَدًا}$$

$$\text{وَّ اَنَّا لَا نَدْرِىٓ اَشَرٌّ اُرِيْدَ بِمَنْ فِى الْاَرْضِ اَمْ اَرَادَ بِهِمْ رَبُّهُمْ رَشَدًا}$$

And we tried to reach the sky, but we found it filled with strong guards and flaming stars. And we used to sit in some of the sitting places thereof to steal a hearing, but he who would (try to) listen now would find a flame lying in wait for him. And that we know not whether there is some evil meant for the people on earth or whether their Lord means to bring them something good. (Jinn:8-10)

Prophets' tests are the most difficult

- We are all tested in this life, but the Prophets' difficulties are much more severe than ours. The hardships (problems) in this life are temporary and ultimately go away, but the reward God promises for facing them with patience, effort, and reliance on God is big.

- In this specific year of sorrow, God told Prophet Muhammad that after this difficulty, ease is about to come.

$$\text{فَاِنَّ مَعَ الْعُسْرِ يُسْرًا ۙ اِنَّ مَعَ الْعُسْرِ يُسْرًا}$$

(O Prophet) With this difficulty, there is ease. Indeed, with this difficulty, there is ease. (Inshirah: 5-6)

- God revealed the incident of Jinns in the Quran to reassure the Prophet that there is nothing wrong with the message or his preaching. It is the hard-heartedness and self-interest of the leaders of Quraysh that keep the people from this message.

And Allah gives life and death

- Death is an undeniable fact of life that no soul can avoid on earth.
- God said in the Quran, "Every soul shall taste death," which means it will only be God who will live forever. At one point in time, everything else will be dead.
- In the Quran, God told us categorically that it is only God who gives life and death.
- We see a person dying due to natural causes, an accident, or a disease, but these are just causes. God planned to take that person back when his/her time was due.
- The length of someone's life is something that is already written in advance by God, and no one can change it.
- God gave us this life, and He can take it back at any time He wishes.
- In Islam, when we hear about the death of someone, we are asked to say the following:

To Allah we belong and to Him we return

- If we trust in God, should we even ask anyone for help?
- What should be a believer's reaction upon losing a loved one?

Chapter 21

Israa and Mairaj

In this chapter, we will study the two miracles given to Prophet Muhammad: Israa (the Night Journey) and Mairaj (Ascension to Heaven).

Th Events of Israa and Mairaj

- *Israa* (Night Journey) and *Mairaj* (Ascension) are two separate incidents, and historians differ on whether both happened on the same night or different nights.
- After the Year of Sorrow and the trial of Ta'if, God blessed the Prophet with a great miracle.
- After seeing the most difficult time in his life, it was only natural that he would be gifted with one of the all-time highs.
- Allah blessed him with one of the greatest miracles, or, in fact, some scholars say, the greatest miracle, that the Prophet has been given as a personal experience.

Special case with the Prophets

- Prophets and messengers are teachers and guides for their nations. For a successful teacher, it is important that they have firsthand experience in the subject they teach; they cannot teach something they are not very familiar with.
- Matters related to religion and life are communicated through the revelation of texts to prophets, such as the Quran.
- God uses unique insight (also called intuition), dreams, or symbolism (things explained symbolically) to communicate certain matters to His prophets:
  - Something related to the next life (unseen).
  - Something significant in this life, but cannot be put into words.
- An example of Symbolism is standing up when the national anthem is played or sung to show respect. It is a symbolic act.
- Also, our physical bodies have limitations: our eyes cannot see beyond a specific limit, and prophets cannot see or comprehend some of these matters physically.
- The special dreams shown to the Prophets are called *Royaa*.

Examples of Symbolism

- To understand how Prophets see things in symbolic dreams, we can turn to two dreams mentioned in Surah Yusuf.
- Prophet Yusuf sees a dream in which eleven stars, the sun, and the moon are making sajdah of respect to him.
- Similarly, the king of Egypt at that time saw in his dream seven slim cows eating seven fat cows, and seven dried crops eating seven green crops.
- **Question:** Do you know what the actual meaning of those dreams was? Discuss in class.

The Message behind Israa and Mairaj

- Before going into the details of the events, let's look into the hidden message behind these events.
- One of the ways God comforted Prophet Muhammad after the year of sorrow was through the incident of Israa and Mairaj. It was glad tidings (good news) for him in the form of a prediction.
- Masjid Al-Haram was the symbol of obedience shown by Prophet Ibrahim and his son, who built it to worship the one true God.
- Masjid Al-Aqsa was the symbol of power given to Prophet Daud and Prophet Suleiman by God and represented the blessings sent to them, who were among the children of Israel (Jews and Christians).
- In the time of the Prophet, Quraysh, and especially the disbelievers, were the guardians of Kabaah, and Jews and Christians were the guardians of the Bait al-Maqdas (Romans had the charge).
- Through the journey of Israa and Mairaj, God wanted to:
  - Announce that the time was about to come when the guardianship of both central places of worship, Makkah/Kabaah and Bait al Maqdas (Jerusalem), would be handed over to the Prophet and his companions, who would be victorious.
  - Threaten the disbelievers (both Quraysh and Jews/Christians) that they would be removed from the status of leadership and would be ruined.

What are Israa and Mairaj?

سُبْحٰنَ الَّذِىٓ اَسْرٰى بِعَبْدِهٖ لَيْلًا مِّنَ الْمَسْجِدِ الْحَرَامِ اِلَى الْمَسْجِدِ الْاَقْصَا الَّذِىْ بٰرَكْنَا حَوْلَهٗ لِنُرِيَهٗ مِنْ اٰيٰتِنَا ؕ اِنَّهٗ هُوَ السَّمِيْعُ الْبَصِيْرُ

"Exalted is He who took His Servant by night from al-Masjid al-Haram to the faraway Mosque (Masjid Al-Aqsa), whose surroundings We have blessed, to show him of Our signs. Indeed, He is All-Hearing, All-Seeing." (Surah Israa or Bani Israel:1)

وَ لَقَدْ رَاٰهُ نَزْلَةً اُخْرٰى عِنْدَ سِدْرَةِ الْمُنْتَهٰى عِنْدَهَا جَنَّةُ الْمَأْوٰى اِذْ يَغْشَى السِّدْرَةَ مَا يَغْشٰى مَا زَاغَ الْبَصَرُ وَ مَا طَغٰى لَقَدْ رَاٰى مِنْ اٰيٰتِ رَبِّهِ الْكُبْرٰى

And he has seen the angel once more coming down near the Lot tree at the very end; there is paradise near it. When the Lot tree was covered with what was covering it. His eyes did not wander or slip, and he saw the great signs of his Lord. (Mention of Mairaj in Suah Najam: 13-18)

- The Prophet went from *Masjid Al-Haram* to *Masjid Al-Aqsa* and returned in a single night.
- As mentioned earlier, it is possible that Mairaj occurred the same night or on another night. The Prophet ascended to the world we are unaware of, known only to God and His angels.
- There is disagreement among the Prophet's earlier companions over whether the journey was physical or spiritual. The Quran referred to it as a dream in Surah Israa, suggesting it was a spiritual experience shown in a *Royaa*.

وَ مَا جَعَلْنَا الرُّءْيَا الَّتِيْ اَرَيْنٰكَ اِلَّا فِتْنَةً لِّلنَّاسِ

And the dream that we have shown you, we have made it a trial for these people (Surah Israa: 60)

A Spiritual Experience

An experience in which the prophets experience something very real (no interpretation is required) or symbolic (interpretation is required) in a dream. An example of real is when the Prophet visited Masjid Al-Haram without physically going there, but he saw and remembered everything that Masjid Al-Aqsa has (it's the actual place where no interpretation is required). An example of symbolism is when, in Masjid Al-Aqsa, he led the prayers, and all the prophets prayed behind him, interpreting that he would be given the religious leadership of the world.

Details of the Incident

- Keep in mind that there is disagreement over whether the journey was physical or spiritual, with the majority of the scholars considering it physical. The details below are regardless of that.

- The Prophet was taken from Masjid Al-Haram to Masjid Al-Aqsa in one night, where he led the prayers, with all the prophets praying behind him.

- This was a sign that Prophet Muhammad now represented all the prophets, and every nation on earth should believe in him, including Jews and Christians.

- On the way to the heavens with Angel Jibrael, Prophet Muhammad was introduced to other prophets, and it appeared that each was stationed at a different level in heaven.

- He was introduced to Adam, Ibrahim, Musa, Haroon, Yousuf, Yahya, and Isa. Some other names also appear in different narrations, such as Idrees.

- All these prophets are somehow related to Masjid Al-Haram and Masjid Al-Aqsa, consistent with the purpose of this journey – E.g., Prophets Musa, Isa, Haroon, Yousuf, and Yahya were all related to Masjid Al-Aqsa.

- Jibrael presented the prophet with two vessels: one with milk and the other with wine. He asked the Prophet to choose one for himself and his nation. The prophet chose milk. Jibrael told him that he had decided what was close to human nature.

- The prophet was shown many rivers and canals in paradise. Two were from this world (the Nile and the Euphrates), and two were from paradise. One of the paradise rivers was Al-Kawthar, which Jibrael said had been given to Prophet Muhammad.

- The word Kawthar means plentiful. This was also a sign that the Kabaah, the source of many blessings on this earth, would be given to Prophet Muhammad. This is also referred to in Surah Al-Kawthar.

(O Prophet) We have bestowed this "Source of Plenty" (meaning Kabaah) on you. So, now (in this house) pray only to your Lord and sacrifice for Him alone. Indeed, your enemy will be cut down, and no one will remember him (Kawthar: 1-3)

- This surah has predictions for the Prophet: The Kabaah would be under the control of the Prophet. Makkah would fall to him. Many people would come within the fold of Islam (by praying and dedicating their sacrifices to the one True God). The enemies of God would be wiped out, and no one would remember them.

- The Prophet also saw Bayt al-Mamur, a house like the Kabaah, up in the heavens. Every day, 70,000 angels circle it, just as we circle the Kabaah. No angel gets a second turn since there are so many of them.

- The prophet went all the way to where this world (that we have access to) ends and another world (that only God and His angels know) begins (to the boundary). This place has a tree that divides the two worlds, called "Sidrat ul Muntaha" (the "Lote Tree" at the very end). God's Kingdom starts there. It is difficult for us, as humans, to perceive it.

- The Prophet was also shown many parts of *Jannah* (Paradise) and *Jahannam* (Hell), along with the people in them. The purpose of showing all this to Prophet Muhammad was to ask about those people and their sins and crimes, so he could warn his people to avoid them (e.g., people who backbite or slander were shown in hell).

How should we approach such events?

- Humans are intelligent creatures, but even though we have created wonders, we still have many limitations.

- We cannot see beyond a specific limit; we cannot see things that do not reflect light or are not within the visible spectrum. Our hearing ability is limited. We cannot perceive things that we have not seen before, and often cannot relate to something that already exists in this world.

- The only source of information about the future and the afterlife is God. He communicates to us through the Quran or the Prophet about such topics.

- God uses the likeness of things from this world to explain life in the hereafter, or else we would have no way of understanding it.

- We must take God's information at face value. We must appreciate what He has told us and try to understand it in the light of our worldly experiences. If something is beyond our understanding, we must let it be rather than pursue it to the end. God guided us about the approach that a believer must take.

- Please focus on the powerful message and lessons that we get from such events.

- Whether it was a physical journey or a spiritual one, it does not diminish the greatness of these events or the miracle given to the Prophet.

- God gave us guidance on how to look at such extraordinary events.

Guidance from the Quran for such events

هُوَ الَّذِىٓ أَنزَلَ عَلَيۡكَ الۡكِتٰبَ مِنۡهُ اٰيٰتٌ مُّحۡكَمٰتٌ هُنَّ أُمُّ الۡكِتٰبِ وَ أُخَرُ مُتَشٰبِهٰتٌ ۖ فَاَمَّا الَّذِيۡنَ فِىۡ قُلُوۡبِهِمۡ زَيۡغٌ فَيَتَّبِعُوۡنَ مَا تَشَابَهَ مِنۡهُ ابۡتِغَآءَ الۡفِتۡنَةِ وَ ابۡتِغَآءَ تَاۡوِيۡلِهٖ ۖ وَ مَا يَعۡلَمُ تَاۡوِيۡلَهٗٓ إِلَّا اللّٰهُ ۖ وَ الرّٰسِخُوۡنَ فِى الۡعِلۡمِ يَقُوۡلُوۡنَ اٰمَنَّا بِهٖ ۖ كُلٌّ مِّنۡ عِنۡدِ رَبِّنَا ۖ وَ مَا يَذَّكَّرُ إِلَّآ أُولُوا الۡاَلۡبَابِ

He is the one who revealed this book to you. In this, some verses are basic; they are the center of the book, while others are allegorical (symbolic). Those people* who have a problem in their hearts follow the allegorical verses, either to create issues in religion, or they are behind things that they cannot perceive. No one knows the reality of such verses except God. People with real knowledge say this is all from our Lord (we don't need to know everything). This is a reminder for intelligent people. (Aal-e-Imran: 7)

*These are not the normal people who want to pursue knowledge in various fields of science, but those religious scholars who want to know more about the unseen. E.g., when God said there would be 19 angels deputed on the Hellfire, they wanted to know why 19? This knowledge is useless because we can never know the reason behind this count.

The Reaction from Quraish

- When Prophet Muhammad told Quraysh and his companions about this event, as expected, he got a mixed reaction.
- The Quraysh started to make fun of it and started propaganda against the Prophet, saying that he had 'lost his mind' and was now daydreaming about ruling over both Bani Ismail and Bani Israel. They called this incident 'a fancy and false desire'.
- Some people, especially those who had visited Masjid Al-Aqsa, wanted to fact-check his statements and asked him to explain the Masjid so they could verify the details.
- It is reported that when the Prophet was telling them about the place, God showed it to him at that time, so he could explain it in detail, so that there would be no chance the Quraysh would deny it.
- Some of the newer Muslims were skeptical about it because they were unable to perceive the idea of the Prophet going to Masjid Al-Aqsa in one night and coming back with such accurate details about it.
- Muslims like Abu Bakr (hence called *As-Siddiq*) and others said that if the Prophet had said so, it must be so, because they had an unshakable belief in the prophethood of the Prophet Muhammad and in his relationship with God. They understood very well that they might have limitations, but God did not.

Israaa and Mairaj in the books of history

- There are hundreds of narrations reported about this incident in the books of history and hadith. Only a few of those narrations provide a broader picture and align with the Quran's objective for this incident.
- When Islam spread among neighboring nations, and people traveled from Makkah and Medina to these lands, some of these narrations were passed on from one generation to another, but the narrator's opinion and comments were all mixed up with the original incident and the details about it.
- Storytelling in the second/third century Hijrah was considered an art and a profession, and storytellers were popular among the masses. They used to exaggerate and fabricate details to make their stories more interesting to listeners.
- There are many versions of the same report, with minor and sometimes significant differences, making it hard to reconcile them.
- Think of this incident as a puzzle with hundreds of pieces scattered all over the place, hard to put together.
- The best approach to understanding such incidents reported in history is to study them in light of the Quran and extract the core message, rather than held up in the details and lose sight of it.
- The purpose of these events is to give glad tidings to Prophet Muhammad and his companions that Islam will be victorious and that Muslims will become the new religious leaders of the world, and that both major places of worship, associated with two great Prophets, will be under Muslim rule.
- Such an approach is valid for all incidents reported from the time of the Prophet.

Lessons for the Muslims

- In the face of all the challenges that Prophet Muhammad faced in the 9th and 10th years of prophethood, Israaa and Mairaj were the best gifts he could get from God. Through this incident, God reminded the Prophet that he was not alone and that He was with him at all times, fully aware of the challenges he was facing in his mission. Patience and perseverance bear fruit, so God gave him the good news about the victories and successes waiting for him and his companions. These glad tidings in the form of predictions did two things:
  - They proved to the addressees of the Quran that Prophet Muhammad was a true prophet of God because only God could predict the future with such authority.
  - It reinforced the faith of the believers, telling them that they were on the right path and that their challenges were temporary. Their patience and perseverance would lead to success in this life, and if they died in the way of Allah, a paradise full of blessings awaited them in the next life.

All-Hearing **All-Seeing**

- These two attributes play a critical role in our faith in God.
- In the Quran, many verses end with these two attributes together.
- In simple terms, these two attributes tell us that God is completely aware of everything that is going on; He hears everything people say or even think; He sees everything, including every act that happens on this earth, including those we cannot see.
- He did not just create the world and us, but He also runs the affairs.
- Sometimes, during difficult times, we tend to think, "Where is God?" "Why is He not doing anything about it?"
- From the example of the Prophet, we should learn that we are asked to play our role with patience and perseverance on the right path, and make dua, and God's help will come at the right time.
- It is the challenges of life that make us strong and grow – if we pay attention to them, God also helps.

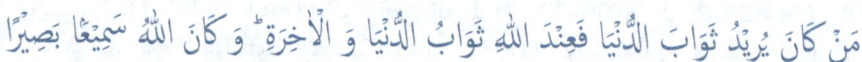

he who wants the reward of this world, it lies with God also; and he who wants the reward of the next world, then with God lies the reward of this world and of the next one as well, and God hears and sees all. (4:134)

SEERAH ACTIVITY

Time to Complete: _____

Instructions: Please print this page and complete it.

ISRAA WAL MAIRAJ WORD SCRAMBLE

RAMEDS

RSOWRO

RIASA

REJUEMLSA

QSLAAA

RAAHTWK

RAPAIESD

RLISEA

IADMNE

GKCABBTINI

Chapter 22

God's help is on the way

In this chapter, we will study the events closer to migration to Medinah that show that God's promised help for Muslims was on the way.

A new home for the Message

Old Yathrib (the now Medina-tun-Nabi) and Local Tribes

- Yathrib was about as far as ten days of journey north of Makkah. Yathrib was renamed Medina after the Prophet Muhammad migrated there. It was named "Medina-tun-Nabi" (The city of the Prophet). Later, it is reduced to Medina.

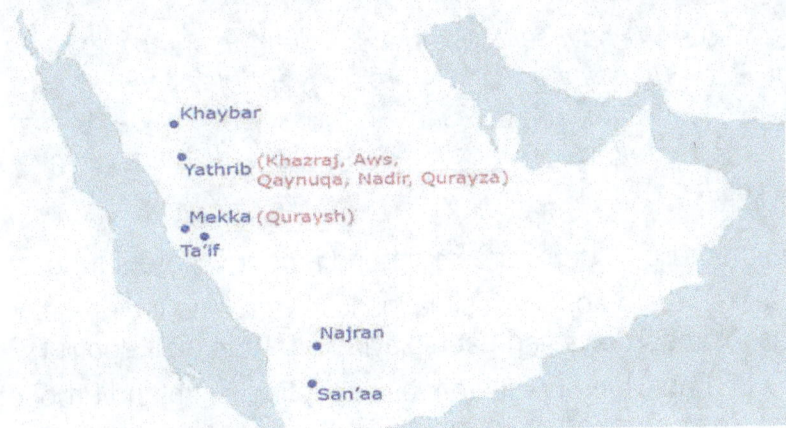

- Two Arab tribes, the Aws and the Khazraj, lived there. They were also idolaters with the same roots as Quraysh.
- A few Jewish tribes were also settled there for a long time. The prominent ones were Banu Nadhir, Banu Qurayzah, and Banu Qaynuqah. Banu Nadhir and Qurayzah were scholars of the Torah.
- They migrated from Palestine in search of the last prophet, which they thought would come in their generation.
- People of the Book (especially Jews) who were aware of the revelation and were considered more knowledgeable had significant influence in this area.
- Aws and Khazraj were idolaters but were aware of the concepts of Tawheed and the Day of Judgment, and idol worship was less prevalent here than in Makkah.
- Some of them even accepted Judaism as their religion.
- Jews were politically very active there, in a negative way, and plotted to damage Aws and Khazraj from the inside to keep hold of the area.
- When some leaders of Aws and Khazraj tried to resist this influence, the Jews advanced their plot, which resulted in many battles between Aws and Khazraj in which they both suffered human and financial losses.
- This resulted in the loss of key leadership on both sides, and there was no one left to stand up against the Jews; both tribes realized this later and started looking for new leadership.

Meeting with a group from Yathrib

- During the 11th year of prophethood, the Prophet met a group from the tribe of Khazraj.
- After mutual consultation, they recognized that Prophet Muhammad was the same prophet that the Jews had been talking about and waiting for – they wanted to take the lead over the Jews in this matter, as the Jews had been threatening them with this new prophet. They told the Prophet:

"O Messenger of God! We have left behind a unique nation, torn apart by infighting and chaos. May God bring them together through your blessings. We shall return to our people and communicate your message to them. We shall call them to the faith which we have accepted. If we can be united, no one shall be more revered and respected than you."

- They realized that religion could create a bond among different tribes.
- The Prophet asked them about the situation in Yathrib and their relationship with the Jews. He was told how Jews had been playing a part in their conflicts.
- The people of Yathrib were hopeful that by accepting Islam and Prophet Muhammad as their prophet, they would gain the upper hand over the Jews and eliminate their subdued situation. The first people who accepted Islam were:

Asad Bin Zurarah and Awf Bin al-Harith from the Banu Najjar; Rafi Bin Malik from the Banu Zurayq; Qutbah Bin Amir Bin Hadidah from the Banu Salamah; Uqbah Bin Amir Bin Nabi from the Banu Haram, and Jabir Bin Abdullah from the Banu Ubaid.

The First Pledge (Promise)

- Remember the verses of Surah Alam-Nashrah. These verses were revealed around the same time that God was preparing the Prophet to leave Makkah and find a new home for Islam.

$$\text{اَلَمْ نَشْرَحْ لَكَ صَدْرَكَ وَ وَضَعْنَا عَنْكَ وِزْرَكَ الَّذِيْ اَنْقَضَ ظَهْرَكَ وَ رَفَعْنَا لَكَ ذِكْرَكَ}$$

$$\text{فَاِنَّ مَعَ الْعُسْرِ يُسْرًا اِنَّ مَعَ الْعُسْرِ يُسْرًا}$$

Did we not expand your chest for you? And removed from you, your burden which was breaking your back. And elevated for you, your remembrance (your name). So, indeed, after this difficulty, there is ease, indeed, after this difficulty, there is ease (Surah Inshirah: 1-6)

- When the people of Khazraj returned, they were able to convince people from other tribes to accept Islam and Prophet Muhammad as their leader.
- During the Hajj in the 12th year of prophethood, 12 people from Yathrib took an oath of allegiance at the hands of the Prophet and vowed to follow the teachings of Islam and support the Prophet when the need arose. Never before had a group of 12 people converted outside Makkah / outside Quraysh.
- The Prophet also sent a young man, Musab Bin Umair, to Yathrib to teach them the Quran, explain Islamic fundamentals, and encourage them to pray as per the Ibrahimic tradition.
- Some groups, including the Jews, were getting uncomfortable with this whole situation, but Musab handled them very diplomatically and presented Islam in the best way possible.
- Yathrib was becoming a fertile land for the growth of Islam. No one could have anticipated at that time that Yathrib, now Medinah, would become the homeland of Islam and the Prophet.
- It is narrated that within a few weeks of Musab's arrival in Yathrib, 40 people had converted. And therefore, the Prophet told them they may establish Salat al-Jumu'ah (Friday prayers).
- And so, the very first Friday sermon in the history of Islam was delivered by Musab. It was delivered in the house of Asad ibn Zurarah, who was hosting Musaab in Yathrib.
- Eventually, every subtribe of the Aws and the Khazraj had at least one Muslim household. There was not a single locality of Yathrib without one or more households that had embraced Islam. And the conversion of two people in particular led to a mass conversion. These two were the up-and-coming leaders of the Aws in the vacuum created by the Battle of *Buath* (scores died in that battle)

Predictions made by the Quran

Prediction about the handing over Kabaah to Muslims

- The Quraysh were very proud of being the guardians and caretakers of the Kabaah; it was the main source of their grandeur and power.
- They were busy convincing leaders of Makkah and Yathrib (leaders from the Jewish tribes) that the Prophet had cut himself away from his people.
- God revealed *Surah Al-Kawthar* to deliver the bad news that this source of blessings (what they had been benefiting from) would soon be handed over to Prophet Muhammad and his companions, and that they would all face a humiliating defeat.
- In this surah, there were four predictions for the Prophet:
  - The Kabaah would be within the control of the Prophet.
  - Makkah would fall to him.
  - Many people would come within the fold of Islam (praying and slaughtering).
  - The enemies of God would be wiped out, and no one would remember them.

(O Prophet) We have bestowed this "Source of Plenty" (Kabaah) to you. So, now (in this house) pray only to your Lord and sacrifice for Him alone. Indeed, your enemy will be cut down, and no one will remember him. (Kawthar: 1-3)

Prediction about the destruction of enemies

- Abu Lahab was the Prophet's uncle and a sworn enemy of the Prophet, leading efforts against him. When the Prophet invited his tribe to Islam in the early days on Mount Safa, it was Abu Lahab who verbally abused him.
- Whenever the Prophet tried to approach visitors or different people about Islam, Abu Lahab always shadowed him, telling people not to listen.
- At the time of the boycott, even though he was from Banu Hashim, he sided with the enemies.
- When Abu Talib died, and he gained more influence, he removed the tribal protection from Prophet Muhammad.
- He was a selfish, harsh, and jealous person who loved collecting wealth by hook or by crook.
- The Quran took him as an example in Surah Masad to announce that the enemies of Islam would be destroyed, their hands would be cut, and they would be doomed to hellfire.

تَبَّتْ يَدَا اَبِیْ لَهَبٍ وَّ تَبَّ ۖ مَاۤ اَغْنٰی عَنْهُ مَالُهٗ وَ مَا کَسَبَ ۖ سَیَصْلٰی نَارًا ذَاتَ لَهَبٍ

وَّ امْرَاَتُهٗ ؕ حَمَّالَةَ الْحَطَبِ ۚ فِیْ جِیْدِهَا حَبْلٌ مِّنْ مَّسَدٍ

"May the hands of Abu Lahab be ruined (his support and protection will be destroyed), and ruined is he. His wealth will not avail him or that which he gained. He will [enter to] burn in a Fire of [blazing] flame. And his wife [as well] - the carrier of firewood. Around her neck will be a rope of [twisted] fiber (meaning she is helping both to burn in the fire of hell). (Surah Masad:1-5)

God Exposes the Wicked Leaders

- Before punishing them, God exposed the leaders of the Quraysh to the public and lifted the veil from the morals and social attitudes of these leaders for people to know their disgusting and nasty character under the garb of religious leadership.

فَلَا تُطِعِ الْمُکَذِّبِیْنَ ۖ وَدُّوْا لَوْ تُدْهِنُ فَیُدْهِنُوْنَ ۖ وَ لَا تُطِعْ کُلَّ حَلَّافٍ مَّهِیْنٍ ۖ هَمَّازٍ مَّشَّآءٍ بِنَمِیْمٍ

مَّنَّاعٍ لِّلْخَیْرِ مُعْتَدٍ اَثِیْمٍ ۖ عُتُلٍّ بَعْدَ ذٰلِکَ زَنِیْمٍ

Then, do not obey the deniers. They wish you would soften your position so they would do the same. And do not obey every worthless habitual swearer, scorner, going about with malicious gossip, a preventer of good, transgressing and sinful, cruel, moreover, and illegitimate pretender (has no solid root) (Qalam:8-13)

اَرَءَیْتَ الَّذِیْ یُکَذِّبُ بِالدِّیْنِ ۖ فَذٰلِکَ الَّذِیْ یَدُعُّ الْیَتِیْمَ ۖ وَ لَا یَحُضُّ عَلٰی طَعَامِ الْمِسْکِیْنِ

Have you seen the one who denies the recompense (payback)? They are the ones who push away the orphans and do not encourage the feeding of the poor (Maun:1-3)

کَلَّا بَلْ لَّا تُکْرِمُوْنَ الْیَتِیْمَ ۖ وَ لَا تَحٰٓضُّوْنَ عَلٰی طَعَامِ الْمِسْکِیْنِ ۖ وَ تَاْکُلُوْنَ التُّرَاثَ اَکْلًا لَّمًّا

وَّ تُحِبُّوْنَ الْمَالَ حُبًّا جَمًّا

No, (your situation is) that you do not give respect to the orphans, and do not encourage each other on feeding the poor, and you devour other people's inheritance, you are passionate about collecting wealth (Fajr:17-20)

The Helper

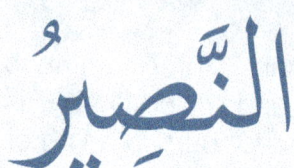

- When God entrusts a person or a group with His mission, He provides His help for their success.
- Such help is provided in the propagation of God's message or at the time when the group is fighting a war with the enemy.
- God's help comes with its own rules and principles.
- What makes a person or a group worthy of God's help is patience, perseverance, piety, and steadfastness in the path.
- In the case of the Messengers, God promises His help for the Messengers and their companions as long as they remain truthful and steadfast.

يَا أَيُّهَا الَّذِينَ آمَنُوا إِن تَنصُرُوا اللَّهَ يَنصُرْكُمْ وَيُثَبِّتْ أَقْدَامَكُمْ

O, who you believe, if you help God, God will help you and strengthen you. (Muhammad:7)

وَكَانَ حَقًّا عَلَيْنَا نَصْرُ الْمُؤْمِنِينَ

Helping the believers is incumbent upon Us. (Rum:47)

SEERAH ACTIVITY

Time to Complete: _____

Instructions: Please print this page and complete it. Otherwise, please take a picture of it, use a drawing tool to draw lines, save it, and print it.

Connect the names of Allah with their meanings.

Ar-Rahman •   • The Creator

Al-Kareem •   • Most Powerful

Ar-Razzaq •   • The Forbearing

As-Samee •   • All-Seer

Al-Wahid •   • Most Merciful

Al-Aziz •   • The Responder

Al-Khaliq •   • The Provider

Al-Mujeeb •   • Most Generous

Al-Haleem •   • The ONE

Al-Baseer •   • All-Hearer

Time to Complete: _____

Instructions: Please print this page and complete it.

Asma ul Husnah Word Search

```
A K Y R M K E A Z W
Z H I K A U D E X A
I A M K A H J O L H
Z B A P H R M E J I
R E L B B A E A E D
A E I S H A L E N B
Z R K L A R S I M L
Z X H A Q M Z E Q T
A X F X Q S E T E F
Q V J H A L E E M R
```

Khabeer	Rahman	Mujeeb	Aziz
Khaliq	Kareem	Baseer	
Malik	Samee	Razzaq	
Haleem	Wahid	Haqq	

Chapter 23

Final Warning and Disassociation

In this chapter, we will study one of the phases of God's Law of Conclusive Arguments in which final warnings to the disbelievers are given, and the Prophet and his companions are asked to disassociate themselves from them.

There is no hope in Makkah

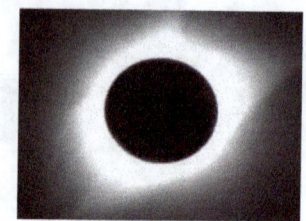

- The Quraysh in Makkah were becoming a hindrance to the propagation of the message of Islam. Although the Prophet had tried every possible way to convince the Quraysh of Islam's message, nothing was working.

- Some people in Quraish thought his migration to another place would be good. Others thought that eliminating him was the only option.

- The mission of the Prophet was reaching a stage where:
  - In Makkah, whoever had the slightest bit of human kindness and goodness in their hearts had already accepted Islam.
  - Some people wanted to accept Islam (or at least accepted Islam in their hearts), but they were weak and did not want to expose their Islam due to backlash.
  - The rest were either rigid in their stance towards Islam and were actively opposing it, or were heedless due to their love for this world and its pleasures.

- The prophet was gradually shifting the focus of his efforts away from Makkah.

- The Prophet also used two of the largest gatherings held around Hajj time, the fair of "Akkaz" and the fair of "Zul Majaz".

- What was happening with Prophet Muhammad was not new. Other Messengers went through the same situation.

قَالَ رَبِّ إِنِّي دَعَوْتُ قَوْمِي لَيْلًا وَّ نَهَارًا ۚ فَلَمْ يَزِدْهُمْ دُعَآءِىٓ إِلَّا فِرَارًا

وَ إِنِّي كُلَّمَا دَعَوْتُهُمْ لِتَغْفِرَ لَهُمْ جَعَلُوٓا أَصَابِعَهُمْ فِىٓ أٰذَانِهِمْ وَ اسْتَغْشَوْا ثِيَابَهُمْ وَ أَصَرُّوا وَ اسْتَكْبَرُوا اسْتِكْبَارًا

ثُمَّ إِنِّي دَعَوْتُهُمْ جِهَارًا ۙ ثُمَّ إِنِّي أَعْلَنْتُ لَهُمْ وَ أَسْرَرْتُ لَهُمْ إِسْرَارًا ۙ فَقُلْتُ اسْتَغْفِرُوا رَبَّكُمْ ۖ إِنَّهُ كَانَ غَفَّارًا

يُّرْسِلِ السَّمَآءَ عَلَيْكُمْ مِّدْرَارًا ۙ وَّ يُمْدِدْكُمْ بِأَمْوَالٍ وَّ بَنِينَ وَ يَجْعَلْ لَّكُمْ جَنَّتٍ وَّ يَجْعَلْ لَّكُمْ أَنْهٰرًا ۙ مَا لَكُمْ لَا تَرْجُونَ لِلّٰهِ وَقَارًا

He (Nuh) said, "My Lord, indeed I invited my people [to truth] night and day. But my invitation only made them run away more than before. And indeed, every time I invited them that You may forgive them, they put their fingers in their ears, covered themselves with their garments, persisted, and were arrogant with [great] arrogance. Then, I invited them publicly. Then I announced to them and [also] advised them secretly. And said, 'Ask forgiveness of your Lord. Indeed, He is Always Forgiving. He will send [rain from] the sky upon you in [continuing] showers, increase your wealth and children, and provide for you gardens and rivers. What is [the matter] with you that you do not attribute to God [due] to the respect (that He deserves) … (Nuh:5-13)

Final General Warning and Disassociation

General warning given to Quraish

- Before migrating to another land, the Prophet Muhammad and his companions were asked to follow specific steps. These steps are discussed here.

- The Quran reminded them on multiple occasions that God honored them by sending a prophet among them, but they did not appreciate it. Therefore, there is no reason to continue like this; the Messenger must move to the next step of his mission, and their punishment is near, as they have been asking for.

- The final warnings were issued in the Quran:

وَ أَقْسَمُوا بِاللهِ جَهْدَ أَيْمَانِهِمْ لَئِنْ جَاءَهُمْ نَذِيرٌ لَيَكُونُنَّ أَهْدَى مِنْ إِحْدَى الْأُمَمِ ۖ فَلَمَّا جَاءَهُمْ نَذِيرٌ مَّا زَادَهُمْ إِلَّا نُفُورًا ۙ اسْتِكْبَارًا فِي الْأَرْضِ وَ مَكْرَ السَّيِّئِ ۚ وَ لَا يَحِيقُ الْمَكْرُ السَّيِّئُ إِلَّا بِأَهْلِهِ ۚ فَهَلْ يَنْظُرُونَ إِلَّا سُنَّتَ الْأَوَّلِينَ ۚ فَلَنْ تَجِدَ لِسُنَّتِ اللهِ تَبْدِيلًا ۖ وَ لَنْ تَجِدَ لِسُنَّتِ اللهِ تَحْوِيلًا

And they swore by God their strongest oaths that if a warner came to them, they would be more guided than [any] one of the [previous] nations. But when a warner came to them, it did not increase them except in hatred. [Due to] arrogance in the land and plotting of evil; but the evil plot does not encompass except its people. Then do they await except the way of the former people? But you will never find in the way of God any change, and you will never find in the way of God any alteration". (Fatir:42-43)

- When people are on the wrong path, God gives them multiple warnings through various means before they face the consequences of their actions.

- It is God's practice to hold us accountable for our bad actions only after He gives us a chance to see and consider the consequences – if we don't pay heed, Satan sometimes helps us do the bad afterward.

Disassociation

- To ensure that, at the time of punishment, Prophet Muhammad and his companions were asked to completely disassociate themselves from the disbelievers and bear no responsibility for their protection or safety.

- Prophet Muhammad announced his dissociation (or acquittal) from his people during the last year of his stay in Makkah. This is mentioned in the Quran in many places:

قُلْ يٰقَوْمِ اعْمَلُوْا عَلٰى مَكَانَتِكُمْ اِنِّىْ عَامِلٌ ۖ فَسَوْفَ تَعْلَمُوْنَ ۙ مَنْ يَّأْتِيْهِ عَذَابٌ يُّخْزِيْهِ وَ يَحِلُّ عَلَيْهِ عَذَابٌ مُّقِيْمٌ

اِنَّآ اَنْزَلْنَا عَلَيْكَ الْكِتٰبَ لِلنَّاسِ بِالْحَقِّ ۖ فَمَنِ اهْتَدٰى فَلِنَفْسِهٖ ۚ وَ مَنْ ضَلَّ فَاِنَّمَا يَضِلُّ عَلَيْهَا ۚ وَ مَآ اَنْتَ عَلَيْهِمْ بِوَكِيْلٍ

"Say, "O my people, work according to your position, [for] I am working, and you will know. To whom will come a torment disgracing him, and on whom will descend an enduring punishment." Indeed, We sent down to you the Book for the people in truth. So, whoever is guided is for [the benefit of] his soul; and whoever goes astray only goes astray to its detriment. And (O Prophet) you are not a manager over them." (Zumr:39-41)

قُلْ يٰٓاَيُّهَا الْكٰفِرُوْنَ لَآ اَعْبُدُ مَا تَعْبُدُوْنَ وَ لَآ اَنْتُمْ عٰبِدُوْنَ مَآ اَعْبُدُ وَ لَآ اَنَا عَابِدٌ مَّا عَبَدْتُّمْ

وَ لَآ اَنْتُمْ عٰبِدُوْنَ مَآ اَعْبُدُ لَكُمْ دِيْنُكُمْ وَلِيَ دِيْنِ

Say, "O disbelievers, I do not worship what you worship. Nor are you worshippers of what I worship. Nor will I be a worshipper of what you worship. Nor will you be worshippers of what I worship. For you is your religion, and for me is my religion." (Kafiroon:1-6)

The Second Pledge of Aqabah

- To completely disassociate, the Prophet and his companions needed to leave this place.

- Due to Musab Bin Umair teaching the Quran/Islam to the people of Yathrib, and to people hearing about the acceptance of Islam by a few Khazraj, occasionally, people would come from Yathrib to Makkah, meet the Prophet, and accept Islam.

- In the 13th year, a group of 75 people from Yathrib came for Hajj, and met the Prophet (secretly), but this time not to accept Islam but to take the Prophet under their protection and invite him to come to Yathrib.

- However, the Prophet could not accept this invitation without receiving instructions from God, as stated earlier, because the Prophets do not decide to leave their nation on their own.

- The Prophet asked them if they would protect him and his family as they protected their wives and sons; he would consider their promise and protection.

- One of the people from Yathrib said, by holding the Prophet's hand, "We are brought up in the midst of battles and know well the arts of archery and fencing and would do everything to protect the Prophet." This pledge was called the Second Pledge of Aqabah.

The Second Pledge - Concerns

- Abbas bin Ubadah Al-Khazraji made a speech at that moment, which is recorded in the books of history.

"O' Khazraj, do you know what the reality of this pledge is? Because of this, you will be required to fight everyone, regardless of race. In this struggle, if you can remain committed to your promise despite losing your wealth and possessions and your honorable men, only then take this step, and if you do so, it will be good for you both in this world and the next. But, if you start thinking that the loss of your wealth is a hardship and the killing of your good men a great loss and that it would be better that you leave the Prophet, then it would be better if you do not take this oath now, because the other option will be a great disgrace for you, both in this world and the next."

- The possibility of war was discussed, and both Aws and Khazraj promised to defend the Prophet with their lives.
- A concern was raised that the Prophet might leave after the Quraysh was defeated, and the Prophet Muhammad promised to stay with them through thick and thin and to accept Yathrib as his new home.
- The Prophet asked them for complete submission: to listen to and obey him under all conditions when carrying out God's commands, and to treat him as their leader in all matters.
- When the group asked, after doing all this for him and Islam, what they would get in return, the Prophet responded, "Paradise."

Reaction of Quraish

- To organize matters in Yathrib, the Prophet appointed a group of 12 people (from Yathrib) to lead efforts in communication, education, and interaction with other tribes in Yathrib.
- When Quraysh heard about this secret meeting, they used their standard techniques of harassment and threats.
- They got hold of Saad Bin Ubadah and brought him to Makkah from Mina, threatened and bullied him, and said that if they protected the Prophet, they would earn the enmity of the Quraysh and would be responsible for the consequences.
- The Prophet had already shown in his dreams that he would soon be migrating to a landlocked area between two rocky places with plenty of date palm trees, and Yathrib fulfilled these signs.

The Permission Given to the Believers

- After hearing about the Prophet's possible migration, the leaders of Quraysh made the lives of Muslims even more difficult.

- The believers were waiting for the good news that would allow them to migrate to Yathrib, when one day the Prophet told them he had seen signs that Yathrib was their new home, and they could start preparing for the migration.

- The Prophet asked them to prepare quietly, either alone or in small groups, to avoid opposition from the Quraysh.

- Abu Salamah Al-Makhzumi was the first person to migrate to Abyssinia. However, he was stopped by his wife's family, the Banu Mughirah, who refused to allow their daughter to leave. Ultimately, the child was taken into Banu Makhzum's custody, and Umm Salamah had to stay back in Makkah while Abu Salamah left for Yathrib. The family was reunited after almost a year of suffering.

- While the Prophet was in Makkah and waiting for the final permission given to him to migrate, he continued to say this dua:

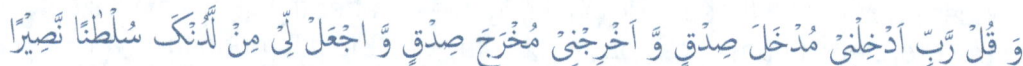

And say: "My Lord! Cause me to enter a safe entrance and to exit a safe exit and grant me from Yourself a supporting authority." (17:80)

- Umar made a plan with Abu Jahal's brothers, Ayyash bin Abi Rabiah and Hisham Bin Abi al-Alas, to migrate. Hisham was locked up in his house by his family and could not reach the meeting place. Umar and Ayyash traveled together and reached Yathrib. Abu Jahal and his brother, Harith Bin Hisham, went after them immediately and told Ayyash that his mother had vowed not to comb her hair or sit in the sun continuously until he returned. As his love for his mother rekindled, Ayyash got ready to leave with his brothers. Umar tried convincing him that this was a plot to get him back, but he disagreed. On the way, his brothers bound him with ropes, took him to Makkah, and locked him in a house. Abu Jahal told the people in Makkah to give the same treatment to their stupid family members as he had to his silly brother.

- When Suhayb Bin Sanan set out for Yathrib, he was stopped. The Idolaters told him that his hands were empty when he came to Makkah. Now that he was leaving, he had a lot of goods. They would not allow him to leave. He asked whether they would let him go if he returned all the wealth. They answered in the affirmative. He gave up whatever he was carrying and migrated to Yathrib empty-handed.

The Plot to Kill the Prophet

- When the believers found another land where they could live and practice Islam peacefully, it kindled hope in their hearts. It appeared to them as moving from the state of a small group persecuted by a powerful enemy to the position of regional leadership with opportunities to grow.

- It is important to note that when Muslims were living under the leadership of the powerful and arrogant Quraysh, they were asked by God to hold their hands and not respond in kind despite all the oppression that the leaders of Quraysh were committing against the Muslims. They were asked to be patient until they moved to a new land where they could have the authority and position to respond to the atrocities of Quraysh.

- However, it was expected that Quraysh would not simply sit and allow all Muslims to migrate to another land and propagate the message of Islam easily. The Muslims were expecting a fierce reaction from them, and the future encounters proved them right. And this is precisely what happened.

- After hearing about the Prophet's possible migration, the leaders of Quraysh met in Dar al Nadwah, and three options were discussed: House-arrest the Prophet, ask him to leave Makkah immediately, or kill him in such a way that no single tribe can be blamed for this act.

- They saw a danger of civil war among tribes if they chose the first option; with the second, the Prophet would still be active and gather force in the new place; hence, the third option was the most appropriate under the circumstances.

- The plan was to get together outside the Prophet's house, and one person from each large tribe would participate in attacking the Prophet as soon as he came out, so no one tribe could be blamed, and no revenge was possible by the Banu Hashim.

- This is God's law that He does not allow any nation to harm His messengers, and they are always taken out safely by God.

- God instructed the Prophet to migrate immediately. The Prophet went to Abu Bakr and told him to accompany him on this journey. He had two camels for this purpose and a confidante, Abdullah Bin Ariqat, to accompany them as a guide for the route to Yathrib. He also took some provisions with him.

- The Cave of Thawr was selected as a temporary shelter on the way from Makkah to Yathrib. He also made arrangements to keep an eye on the movement of Quraysh, who will be following him soon.

The Best Judge

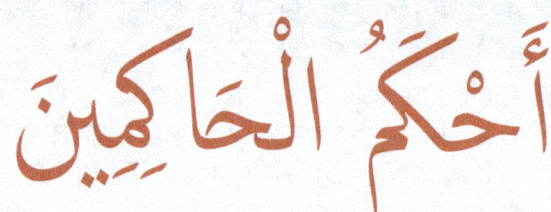

- God is the one who keeps an eye on the bigger picture of this world and our lives, with total knowledge of them, and He is the one who fixes all matters and deals with them fairly and impartially.

- God has said many times in the Quran that He never commits injustice against people; it's always the people who are unjust to themselves.

- Sometimes we may not understand God's judgment in some issues, but His judgments contain many hidden divine purposes we cannot see.

- Quraysh missed the point drastically: that God controls everything and that His judgment will always be the final.

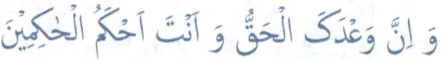

There is no doubt that your promise is true, and you are the best of the Judges (Surah Hud:45)

SEERAH ACTIVITY

Time to Complete: _____

Instructions: Please print this page and complete it.

Fill in the blanks with appropriate words:

1. _____ are God's chosen people who give good news and warning to people.

2. _____ means to put divine words into the heart.

3. The nation of a _____ is punished in this world if it disobeys him.

4. Dawud was a _____.

5. Prophet Muhammad is the _____ prophet of God.

6. Prophet Musa was given the book of _____.

7. Prophet _____ is considered the father of many prophets.

8. The children of Ibrahim were settled in _____ and _____.

9. Prophet Muhammad is from the family of Prophet _____.

10. The name of Baytullah is _____.

11. Prophet _____ came before Prophet Muhammad and told about him.

12. The people of old Makkah were _____ worshippers.

13. The two other main groups in the Arabian Peninsula were _____ and _____.

14. Banu Nadhir was a _____ tribe.

15. The three creations of Allah are: _____, _____, and Angels.

Jews	Ismail	Torah	Palestine	Kabaah	Rasool	Nabi	Jewish	Idol
Ibrahim	Humans	Wahi	Prophets	Makkah	Jinns	Isa	Final	Christians

SURAH MEMORIZATION

The following Surahs were revealed before the migration of Prophet Muhammad, when the final warning was given to the Quraish who rejected Prophet Muhammad (SAW). Memorize one of these Surahs.

1. **Surah Al-Kaafiroon** – The Prophet was told that your job of preaching in Makkah is almost over.

2. **Surah An-Nasr** – The Prophet was given good news that good times will come.

3. **Surah Al-Lahab** – The Prophet was told that Allah's enemies would be punished soon.

4. **Surah Al-Kauther** – The Prophet was given good news that in a few years, the Kabaah will be under his control.

Instructions

- Memorize and recite the Surah with Tajweed.
- Once memorized, record a video with you reciting the Surah.
- Submit the recording via Google Classroom.

Chapter 24

The Migration (*Hijrah*)

In this chapter, we will study one of the most significant events in the history of Islam, and that is the migration from Makkah to Medina.

The Great Migration

Permission to Migrate

- Quraysh surrounded the Prophet's house the same night when they finalized their decision to kill him.

- God told the Prophet in advance of the Quraysh's intention, and he migrated immediately.

- The Prophet instructed Ali to spend the night at his house and settle his matters, as he had other people's belongings that were required to be handed over to their owners.

- He asked Abu Bakr to get ready, and they both moved to the cave of Thawr on the mountain of Thawr, south of Makkah.

- When he left the house, he threw a handful of sand over those besieging his home, and no one could see him going – a miracle from God.

وَ اِذْ يَمْكُرُ بِكَ الَّذِيْنَ كَفَرُوْا لِيُثْبِتُوْكَ اَوْ يَقْتُلُوْكَ اَوْ يُخْرِجُوْكَ ۚ
وَ يَمْكُرُوْنَ وَ يَمْكُرُ اللّٰهُ ۚ وَ اللّٰهُ خَيْرُ الْمٰكِرِيْنَ

And remember (O Prophet) when the disbelievers were plotting against you to either detain you or kill you or expel you from the land. They were planning, and God was planning, and God is the best planner. (Anfal:30)

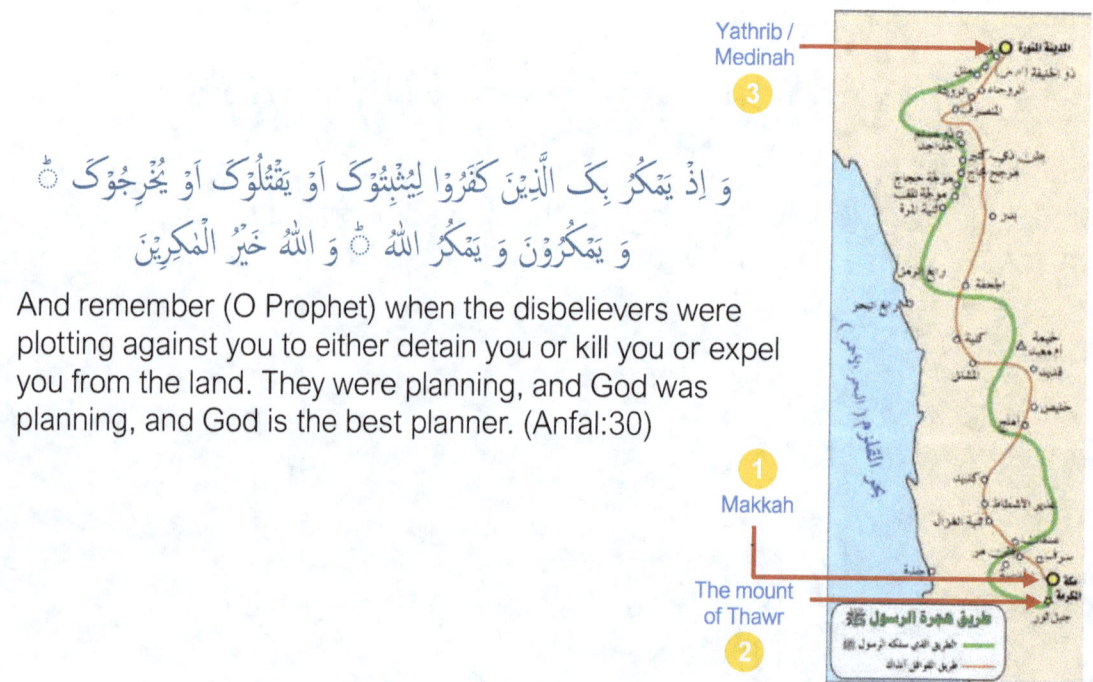

Yathrib / Medinah

3

Makkah

1

The mount of Thawr

2

His companion in the journey

- When Muslims were permitted to migrate, Abu Bakr asked the Prophet to migrate, and the Prophet told him he hoped he would get permission, too, so they could embark on this journey together.
- God told the Prophet to take Abu Bakr as his companion for this long and rough journey, during which he was expecting the evil pursuit by the Quraysh.
- Abu Bakr was very pleased to hear this. He told him he had been looking forward to this moment for months. He has prepared two camels specifically to carry them to Yathrib (camels need to store fat and drink lots of water to get ready for long journeys). The Prophet agreed to take one only if he would pay for the camel.
- Abu Bakr was one of the Prophet's companions who was always the "first" in everything related to Islam and human goodness.
- He was very close to the Prophet even before Islam. The mother of the believers, Ayesha, narrated: "I don't remember any day except the Prophet would come visiting us in our house."

If I were to choose a best friend, I would have definitely chosen Abu Bakr, but he is my brother and my companion, and God has taken your brother and companion (meaning the Prophet himself) as a friend. (Sahih Muslim: 2383)

Staying in the Cave of Thawr

- When the Prophet and Abu Bakr moved to the cave of Thawr, the Quraysh sent horsemen in pursuit around Makkah, near Yathrib.
- The Quraysh announced a reward of 100 camels for anyone who would bring them dead or alive.

On the way to Thawr, several people on the outskirts of Makkah recognized Abu Bakr but not the Prophet. When they asked Abu Bakr, who was with him, he told them, "He is the one who is showing me the way," which was true because the Prophet guided him in Islam.

- They stayed there for three nights, and as per the plan, the following people helped them:
  - **Abdullah, the son of Abu Bakr**, was tasked with bringing food to the cave, keeping an eye on expeditions going out to hunt, and paying attention to any plans or conversations in the marketplace.
  - **Amir Bin Fuhayra, the freed slave of Abu Bakr**, went out with his flocks of sheep and erased the footsteps of the Prophet, Abu Bakr, and Abdullah.
  - **Abdullah bin Ariqat** was their guide, responsible for leading them to Yathrib along a path unknown to the Quraysh.

The incident of Suraqah

- Some greedy people tried their luck and went out to search, including Suraqah bin Malik. He reported his search after he accepted Islam.
- He rode on his warhorse and took his bows and arrows with him in case he faced them.
- He noticed two camels far away and started to follow them. When he was close, his horse stumbled multiple times and got stuck in the sand up to its ankles. He realized that another force beyond this world was helping the Prophet.
- He called them out, assuring them that he would not harm them and that they should allow him to come closer.
- When he was about to turn back, the Prophet said, "O Suraqah, how will you be on the day when you put on the bracelets of Kisra (the Persian Emperor)?" Suraqah was shocked to hear that and asked, "Kisra, the son of Hormuz?!"

- In 636 AD, the battle of Qadisiyyah was fought between Muslims and the army of the Persian Empire, and the victory of Muslims opened the doors of Iraq, Khurasan, and Turkestan for Muslims.

- After the Battle of Qadisiyyah, all the treasures were gathered and sent to Umar, the Caliph at that time. It is said that when the booty was distributed, Suraqah got the beautiful bracelets of Kisra, and he remembered that moment when the Prophet had predicted it a long time ago.

The Trust in God

- The cave of Thawr was a small hiding place for two people, and they were hiding almost at the mouth of the cave.
- One time, they noticed that the people of Quraysh were going up and down the mountain where the cave was located. Abu Bakr was worried, not for his life. He was more concerned about the Prophet because the Quraysh had already decided to kill him, and it was only due to God's help that they could not act on their decision.
- He looked at the Prophet and whispered, "O Prophet of God, if they just look down at their feet level now, they will see us." The Prophet responded to him calmly, and that incident is recorded in the Quran:

$$ اِلَّا تَنْصُرُوهُ فَقَدْ نَصَرَهُ اللهُ اِذْ اَخْرَجَهُ الَّذِينَ كَفَرُوا ثَانِيَ اثْنَيْنِ اِذْ هُمَا فِى الْغَارِ $$

$$ اِذْ يَقُولُ لِصَاحِبِهِ لَا تَحْزَنْ اِنَّ اللهَ مَعَنَا $$

What if you don't help the Prophet – God had already helped him when those who have disbelieved had driven him out of (Makkah), as one of the two (the Prophet), when they were in the cave, said to his companion, "Do not grieve. Indeed, Allah is with us." (Surah Tawbah: 40)

Reaching Quba/Qiba

- It took them around seven days to reach the suburbs of Yathrib, a place called Quba or Qiba. It was a festive occasion in Quba, and the people opened their hearts to the Prophet.
- It is said that every day, they would sit on the ground for hours, staring at the path from Makkah, waiting for the Prophet to appear.
- Many people mistook Abu Bakr for the Prophet. Later, when Abu Bakr used his cloth sheet to cover the Prophet from the sun, they realized their mistake.
- A man saw from a hill that some travelers were on their way. He said aloud, "O' People, he for whom you were waiting has arrived."
- He stayed temporarily at the house of Awf's leader, Kulthum bin Haddam.
- After a two-week stay in Quba, the Prophet proceeded toward Yathrib and led the Friday prayers at the village of Banu Salim.
- Various tribes on the way requested him to stay with them, but he said that God would decide where my camel would stop – to avoid hurting anyone's feelings.

The Jews in this area also came to meet the Prophet, and after meeting him, they went back and confirmed that this was the same Prophet who was foretold in their books, but they could not accept him and would oppose him.

Masjid Quba/Qiba – The First Mosque

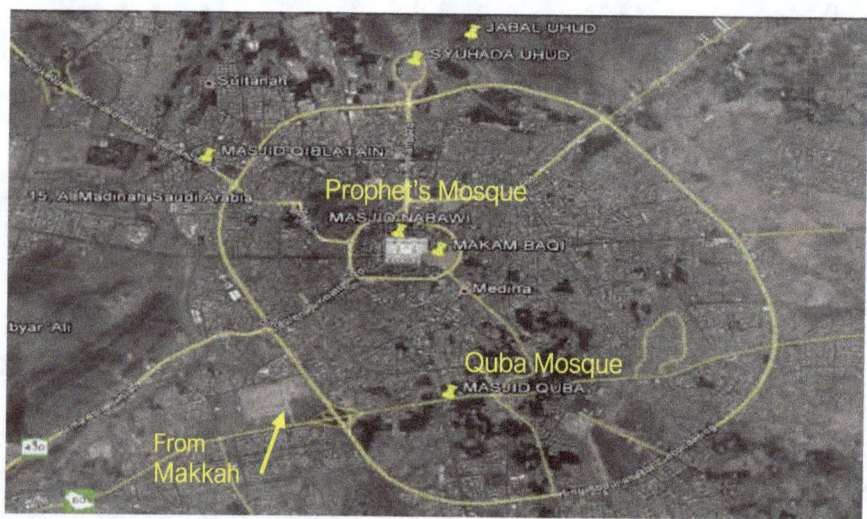

- Using one of the wastelands that belonged to Kulthum (where he stayed), he laid the foundation of the first mosque after the Prophet's arrival, called Masjid Al-Quba.

$$لَا تَقُمْ فِيهِ أَبَدًا ۚ لَمَسْجِدٌ أُسِّسَ عَلَى التَّقْوَى مِنْ أَوَّلِ يَوْمٍ أَحَقُّ أَنْ تَقُومَ فِيهِ ۚ فِيهِ رِجَالٌ يُحِبُّونَ أَنْ يَتَطَهَّرُوا ۚ وَ اللهُ يُحِبُّ الْمُطَّهِّرِينَ$$

Do not stand in this masjid (Masjid Dhirar), the only mosque that deserves your standing, which is the one whose foundation was built on righteousness (Masjid Quba). There are people in it who value purity, and God loves those who strive for it. (Surah Tawbah: 108)

Abdullah Bin Salam

- Not all Jews reacted the same way. Abdullah Bin Salam was a wealthy and learned Jew who lived near Quba.
- When he heard about a Prophet in Makkah, he took a keen interest in the reports of his appearance and researched him from his books.
- When he heard about the Prophet's arrival in Quba, he set out to see him in person.
- He saw people assembled at a place, and the Prophet was speaking. He heard him saying:

"O, People! Spread Salam (Peace), share food (with the poor), pray during the night while people sleep, and you will enter Paradise in Peace." (Tirmidhi, Ibn Majah)

- When Abdullah bin Salam heard these words and looked at the Prophet, he said to himself, "That is not the face of a liar," and he immediately accepted Islam.
- It is said that he told his immediate family about the conversion but kept his Islam secret at the beginning from his Jewish tribe, including the scholars of Jews in the tribe, who were not very happy with this situation.
- Jews of Medina later played a very negative role in the struggle between Islam and its enemies.

Hijrah is not relocation

- The migration (Hijrah) should not be considered a relocation effort by the Prophet and Muslims from one place to another.
- It was a migration from a land where practicing religion and doing good, in general, was difficult to a land where they were free to worship God. This is applicable to us even today.
- Living in an era when practicing religion is not a challenge is a blessing from God, and we should all be grateful to God for it and value this blessing by first practicing Islam and then inviting others to this goodness.
- It also highlights the patience and perseverance of the Prophet and early Muslims through difficult times. It demonstrated to the people of faith that they should never lose hope in the Mercy and Help of God.

Yathrib ⟹ Medina

- The camel of the Prophet finally stopped at a place that belonged to Banu Malik Al-Najjar. The Prophet stayed at an adjacent house that belonged to Abu Ayyub Ansari for the next seven months.

- The Prophet did not like bad names. He changed the names of many companions because their names were somehow associated with polytheistic beliefs.

- The same thing happened with Yathrib. When he arrived here, he changed the city's name because the word Yathrib carries a negative connotation of blame.

- He changed the name to "Al-Medinat un Nabi," "the City of the Prophet," which became Medinah in short.

- In many narrations attributed to the Prophet, the virtues of Medinah are described, indicating that God chose this city for the Prophet and Islam. According to one narration, he started seeing this city in his dreams one year before the migration.

Prophet's love for the city of Medinah

- In Sahih Bukhari, it's narrated that the Prophet made dua for Madinah: "O Allah, cause us to love Madinah as much as we love Makkah, or even more."

- The Prophet also made dua that Madinah be blessed — he said, "O Allah, give us barakah ... in this city of ours." And in Bukhari, he said, "O Allah, Your servant Ibrahim declared Makkah a Haram; and I too am Your servant, so I make dua that You make Madinah a Haram."

- And Ibn Abbas narrates that whenever the Prophet returned from an expedition and saw the line of Madinah in the distance, he would become excited and tell his camel or horse to go faster.

The Subtle and All-Knowing

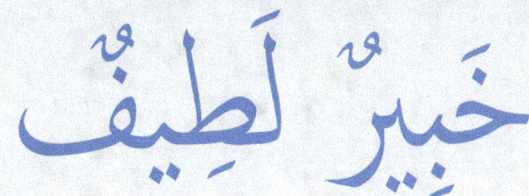

- These two attributes usually come together because God is All-Knowing, and He even knows the subtle things that we can't notice or see/hear.
- God knows all – the hidden and the open, the secret and the obvious, what's done in the day and what's done during the night – nothing escapes Him.
- Sometimes, His help is also very subtle, and it comes through means and ways that we can't comprehend.
- The way God guided the Prophet out of Makkah shows that He is aware of the most minor details we humans ignore.
- Luqman explained these attributes to his son:

يٰبُنَىَّ اِنَّهَآ اِنْ تَكُ مِثْقَالَ حَبَّةٍ مِّنْ خَرْدَلٍ فَتَكُنْ فِى صَخْرَةٍ اَوْ فِى السَّمٰوٰتِ اَوْ فِى الْاَرْضِ يَأْتِ بِهَا اللّٰهُ ۗ اِنَّ اللّٰهَ لَطِيْفٌ خَبِيْرٌ

O my son, if there is an act which is equal to the size of a mustard seed and if that act is done in a deep rock or anywhere in the heavens or on the earth, God will bring it out. Indeed, God is Subtle and All-Knowing. (Luqman:16)

SEERAH ACTIVITY

Create a Makki Seerah Timeline

Instructions

1. Create a visual timeline of Seerah (Makki or Madani or both periods) using:
   a. Index cards
   b. Poster
   c. Digital tools like Canva or Google Slides
2. You can draw, paste pictures, or write short summaries for key events.
3. Specify the period of the timeline.
4. Identify key events that you consider important.
5. Events must be in the correct time order.
6. Mark the approximate date and specific location for the events.
7. Make it visually appealing.

Chapter 25

The Significance of Hijrah

In this chapter, we will study why Hijrah is one of the most significant events in the history of Islam and what lessons we can learn from it.

The Importance of Migration (Hijrah)

- In the eyes of Muslim historians, the Hijrah (the 622 CE migration from Mecca to Medina) is not an "escape from injustice". It is the single most significant turning point in Islamic history. It marks the shift from Islam as a persecuted religion to the start of a vibrant civilization.

- The Hijrah shifted the center of Islamic activity to Medina, an important location that allowed the faith to expand its influence across the Arabian Peninsula.

- Historians view this as the beginning of a global mission, moving from local preaching to a message that would eventually reach major world empires like Byzantium and Persia.

Why did God ask the Prophet to migrate?

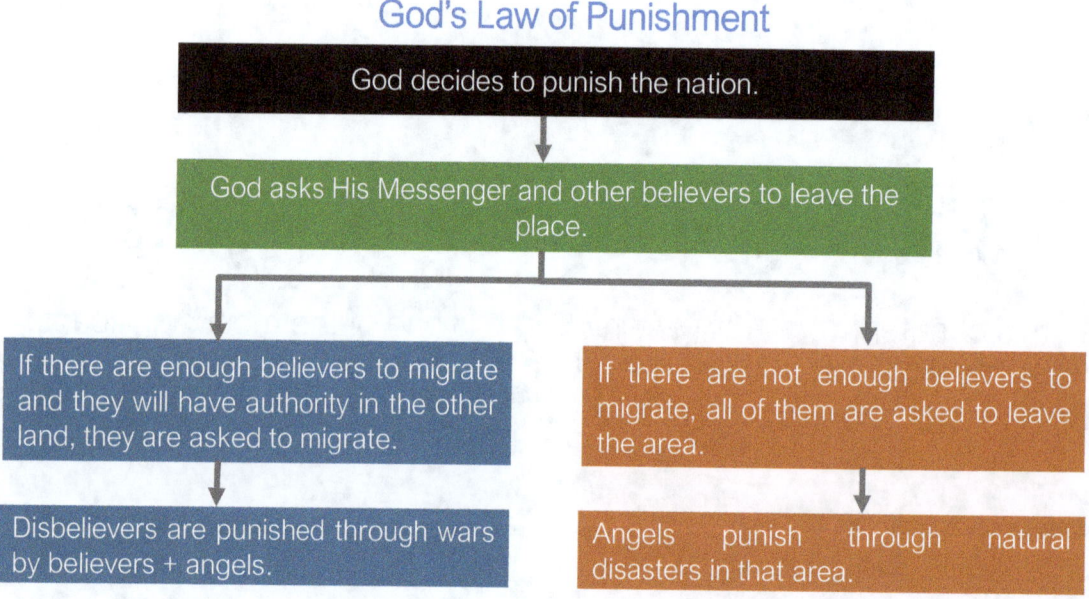

- When the Messengers come to a nation, they are given a choice to accept the message or not until the last moment before the time of punishment.

- All arguments and reasons are given to support the message's truth; all questions are answered; and sometimes mighty miracles and signs are also shown to confirm that the Messenger is from God.

- For all human beings, if they deliberately deny the valid message of God, the decision on their fate is left until the day of judgment.

- For the nations of the Messengers, the decision about their fate is not postponed until the day of judgment; the final decision is made in this world, providing physical proof of God's existence and His Message.

Why did the divine punishment not come immediately?

- The reason for the migration was the ill behavior that disbelievers showed towards the believers, and to remove the believers from harm's way.

- For God to punish the people who have rejected the Messenger, it is required that every believer must leave their place and go to another land.

- **First:** In the 13 years of preaching in Makkah, many people accepted Islam. However, not all of them were able to migrate. Quraysh was able to force some of the relatives (especially financially and socially weak, like women and children) who were hiding their Islam to remain in Makkah.

- The Prophet's daughter, Zaynab, who was married, was not allowed to leave. Similarly, Abu Jahal's brother was tricked into coming back to Makkah and confined in an empty house.

- **Second:** Several people did not find the courage to accept Islam in Makkah due to societal pressure, but in their hearts, they were convinced about the truth of Islam.

- **Third:** For believers to fight the disbelievers after the migration to punish them, it was necessary that they become a large collective strength, and this was only possible if they spread their message in a peaceful environment like Medina, which would take some time.

- The situation in Makkah is depicted in the picture below.

- This situation was not suitable for imposing any punishment on the disbelievers in Makkah, which explains why God did not punish them and waited for the Battle of Badr before the first punishment was given to the leaders of Quraish.

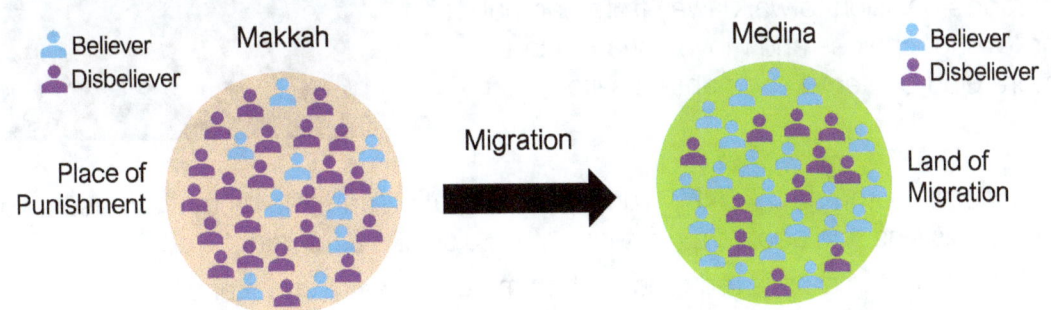

When does migration become mandatory?

- We learned about one type of migration that occurred during the times when the Messengers of God were sent.
- When God's Messengers are present, and there is a place to migrate, and if the person still does not migrate for no apparent reason, then he/she sins in the sight of God.
- There are other times, when the Messenger of God is not present, it is also mandatory for a person to migrate if the following conditions are met:
    - It becomes difficult for a person to worship God.
    - The person is punished for his/her religious beliefs.
    - It becomes a life-threatening situation.
    - He/she has a legal option to move out and relocate to another land.
- In Islamic terms, this is called Hijrah or Migration.
- God does not want people to continue to suffer in a place if they have the option to move to another place.
- God has promised that people who migrate to other lands to worship God will find His earth vast, and they will find the portion of their provisions there from the blessings of God.

A new meaning to the concept of migration

- The Hijrah isn't just a historical story. It also has a personal, religious meaning: it represents a person's decision to walk away from bad habits or "wrong" choices and move toward a better, more God-centered and righteous life.

- Prophet Muhammad used this concept of migration and told us that a person who leaves his sins and adopts a righteous life is also like a migrant.
- This type of migration is required all the time under all circumstances.

Migration vs Relocation

Rule we learned: It is the law of God that when He decides to punish a nation because of its rebellious behavior, He asks the Messenger and his companions to leave the place and settle in another place. Let's look at the circumstances that caused Prophet Muhammad to migrate.

- The leaders of the Quraysh became harsher on Muslims day by day, and the Prophet had the responsibility to save his fellow Muslims from the most brutal of punishments just because they called God their Lord alone.

- The Quraysh had surrounded his house and were ready to kill him.

- The Prophet did not migrate to Medina of his own free will. The Prophet could not decide when to migrate until God granted permission, and he was asked to take Abu Bakr with him.

- He firmly stood by his faith, forsaking his birthplace and homeland, his family, his tribe, his wealth, and his property for the sake of God.

- He took the risk of living in a strange place in a tribal society where he and other Muslims had to begin their lives anew.

- He promised them that he would never leave that land, no matter what.

- The migrants had to leave their entire belongings, homes, wealth, cattle, merchandise, etc in Makkah and arrived in Medinah in a state of poverty and need (almost like a beggar with no means to even eat).

- The new place became dear to their hearts, and they became loyal to that land more than their birthplaces.

الَّذِينَ أُخْرِجُوا مِنْ دِيَارِهِمْ بِغَيْرِ حَقٍّ إِلَّا أَنْ يَقُولُوا رَبُّنَا اللهُ

"[They are] those who have been evicted from their homes without right - only because they say: "Our Lord is God." (Hajj:40)

الَّذِينَ يَقُولُونَ رَبَّنَا أَخْرِجْنَا مِنْ هَٰذِهِ الْقَرْيَةِ الظَّالِمِ أَهْلُهَا ۖ وَ اجْعَلْ لَنَا مِنْ لَدُنْكَ وَلِيًّا ۖ
وَّ اجْعَلْ لَنَا مِنْ لَدُنْكَ نَصِيرًا ۖ

"Our Lord, take us out of this city of oppressive people and appoint for us from Yourself a protector and appoint for us from Yourself a helper?" (Nisa:75)

Hijri, The Lunar Calendar

- Islamic months existed even before the time of Prophet Muhammad.
- Pre-Islamic Arabs used the same 12 lunar month names found in the modern Islamic calendar today (e.g., Ramadan, Muharram, and Rajab)
- Pre-Islamic Arabs practiced adding an extra month to synchronize the lunar calendar with the solar calendar. This practice was called "Nasi". The Quran also mentions that.
- Prophet Muhammad abolished the practice of Nasi toward the end of his life, making the Islamic calendar strictly lunar. This is why Islamic months now "drift" through different seasons every year. For example, because of this, the month of Ramadan falls in all seasons.
- However, there was no concept of a year like in the Christian Calendar. For example, Prophet Muhammad was born in 570 AD.
- In the old days, people used to remember dates by the events – for example, Prophet Muhammad was born in the year when the incident of elephants happened.
- In the time of Caliph Omar, when the Muslim rule was extended, they needed a way to determine the exact date of the year.
- The Prophet's migration was the turning point in the religion of Islam. Muslims moved from a state of oppression to a state of authority and dignity. Omar chose the event of Hijra as the first year of the Islamic Lunar Calendar.
- Since that time, we now have an Islamic calendar. In 2025 AD, it is 1447 AH, read as "After Hijrah".

Lessons learned from Hijrah

- **Plan:** When considering something that requires effort and planning, plan it well in advance and use all available means. When Prophet Muhammad told Abu Bakr that he would be his companion, Abu Bakr began planning. Even if God approves something and His help is included, that does not mean we do not need to prepare.

- **Companionship:** Pick the right companion for the right job, and remember that righteous companionship makes your task easier. Prophet Muhammad chose the person he trusted the most (maybe God guided him on this as well). Traveling puts people outside their everyday routines and comfort zones, creating a "mini-test" for compatibility and problem-solving skills that might not appear in everyday life.

- **Trust:** When you are on the right path (doing the right thing, not just religious), trust in God and His help. The rule of trust in God is that you put your best efforts possible and leave the results in the hands of God.

- **Be Optimistic:** Always approach with optimism; remember, with every difficulty, there is an ease (in fact, many eases around us) after that. Work within the possibilities and towards improving your situation without losing hope. Don't wait for an ideal situation that never occurs.

- **Be Considerate:** When you are in a difficult situation, don't just think of yourself; be considerate of others who are facing the same problem. Empathy and sacrifice are the two attributes that one should strive for in these circumstances.

- **Be Grateful and Reciprocate:** If someone helps you in difficult times, be grateful and return the favor. People who help in times of need are the most precious people whom we should treasure.

- **Look at the bigger picture:** This life is just a small piece of a big picture and should be seen alongside life in the Hereafter. We should never aim to fail in this life, but sometimes if it happens, we should remember that even if we lose in this world, we will win in the Hereafter.

SEERAH BOARD GAME

Create a playable board game that guides players through the major events of the Makki Seerah, teaching them valuable lessons and facts along the way.

Instructions

1. Create on a poster or Canva.
2. Pick a winding trail or spiral/circular path.
3. Create 25-30 squares on the board.
4. Each square should be an event, a question, or an action. Be respectful when creating questions and actions.
5. Create at least 6-8 Makki Seerah events.
6. Add a few Names of Allah on special squares (bonus point or something)
7. Create Question, Challenge, or Action Cards.
8. Add Move Forward and Miss a Turn Cards.
9. Add symbols (Kabaah, desert, etc.)
10. Success Criteria: Complete the Seerah Trail to Medina
11. Play and test it.
12. The activity can be completed in Groups.

Step by Step: How to Create a Board Game Using Canva

https://www.youtube.com/watch?v=z6o5COWZqko

www.ingramcontent.com/pod-product-compliance
Lightning Source LLC
Chambersburg PA
CBHW081326120626
46546CB00011B/3235